D0484872

THE COLLECTED POEMS
OF THEODORE ROETHKE

BY THEODORE ROETHKE

Collected Poems
The Far Field
I Am! Says the Lamb
Words for the Wind
The Waking
Praise to the End!
The Lost Son and Other Poems
Open House
Straw for the Fire: From the Notebooks of Theodore Roethke
1943–63 *selected and arranged by David Wagoner*

FOR CHILDREN:

Party at the Zoo

SELECTED PROSE:

On the Poet and His Craft
edited by Ralph B. Mills, Jr.

SELECTED LETTERS OF THEODORE ROETHKE
edited by Ralph B. Mills, Jr.

THE COLLECTED POEMS
of THEODORE ROETHKE

ANCHOR PRESS
Doubleday
NEW YORK   LONDON   TORONTO   SYDNEY   AUCKLAND

An Anchor Book
Published by Doubleday, a division of
Bantam Doubleday Dell Publishing Group, Inc.,
666 Fifth Avenue, New York, New York 10103

Anchor, Doubleday and the portrayal of an
anchor are trademarks of Doubleday, a division of
Bantam Doubleday Dell Publishing Group, Inc.

Anchor Books edition: 1975

ISBN: 0-385-08601-6

Many of the poems in this collection appeared originally in *The New Yorker* and *Poetry*. Others appeared in *The New York Times*, *The Nation*, *Saturday Review*, NIGHT CROW, Copyright 1944 by Saturday Review Association, Inc., *The Atlantic Monthly*, THE DANCE, Copyright 1952 by the Atlantic Monthly Company, THE EXULTING, HIS WORDS, MEMORY, THE WALL, WHAT NOW?, Copyright © 1956 by Atlantic Monthly Co., *Yale Review*, *The American Scholar*, BIG WIND, Copyright 1947 by The United Chapters of Phi Beta Kappa, *The New Republic*, CARNATIONS, CHILD ON TOP OF A GREEN HOUSE, FLOWER-DUMP, WEED PULLER, MOSS-GATHERING, Copyright 1946 by Editorial Publications, Inc., ELEGY, LOVE'S PROGRESS, "THE SHIMMER OF EVIL," SLUG, Copyright © 1955 by New Republic, Inc., *The Virginia Quarterly Review*, *The Commonweal*, DOUBLE FEATURE AS EPISODE SEVEN, Copyright 1942 by Commonweal Publishing Co., Inc., *The Tiger's Eye*, A FIELD OF LIGHT, Copyright 1948 by The Tiger's Eye, *The Sewanee Review*, JUDGE NOT, Copyright 1947 by The University of the South, *Harper's Bazaar*, MY PAPA'S WALTZ, Copyright 1942 by Hearst Magazines, Inc., and LAST WORDS, Copyright 1946 by Hearst Magazines, Inc., *Harper's*, OLD FLORIST, Copyright 1946 by Harper & Brothers, *American Mercury*, PICKLE BELT, Copyright 1943 by The American Mercury, Inc., *Partisan Review*, *Botteghe Oscure*, THE OTHER, Copyright © 1956 by Botteghe Oscure, HER BECOMING, Copyright © 1958 by Botteghe Oscure, *The Hudson Review*, *The Kenyon Review*, I WAITED, Copyright © 1956 by Kenyon College, *Poems in Folio*, *Flair*, *Landmarks and Voyages*. The Poetry Society Supplement for 1957, *Poetry London-New York*, *Encounter*, *New World Writing*, *Ladies' Home Journal*, *Poetry Northwest*, *New Poems by American Poets, No. 2*, *The Pocket Book of Modern Verse*, *Folkways Album No. FL 9736*, and *Critical Quarterly*.

Contents

OPEN HOUSE 1941

I

II

vi

THE LOST SON AND OTHER POEMS 1948

I

II

III

IV

from PRAISE TO THE END! 1951

I

II

from THE WAKING 1953

from WORDS FOR THE WIND 1958

I *Lighter Pieces and Poems for Children*

II *Love Poems*

ix

THE FAR FIELD 1964

I *North American Sequence*

II *Love Poems*

III *Mixed Sequence*

IV *Sequence, Sometimes Metaphysical*

PREVIOUSLY UNCOLLECTED POEMS

Note

This volume contains all the poems from previous books by Theodore Roethke, except *Party at the Zoo*, which was written expressly for children. There are as well sixteen previously uncollected poems, selected from a considerable number of unpublished poems. These additional pieces, dating from 1943 to 1962, are arranged in approximate chronological order.

In *The Far Field*, the sections entitled "North American Sequence" and "Sequence, Sometimes Metaphysical" are, in content and order, as arranged by Theodore Roethke in the original manuscript. The other sections in that book were altered slightly to withhold for later publication two of the pub songs, "The Saginaw Song" and "Gob Music"—pieces that did not seem appropriate in a last book of poems—and to add "Wish for a Young Wife" and "The Tranced," one of the last poems Theodore Roethke wrote.

I am greatly indebted to several friends of my husband, and to Frank Jones and Stanley Kunitz in particular, for their valuable advice and suggestions.

BEATRICE ROETHKE

OPEN HOUSE

1941

OPEN HOUSE

My secrets cry aloud.
I have no need for tongue.
My heart keeps open house,
My doors are widely swung.
An epic of the eyes
My love, with no disguise.

My truths are all foreknown,
This anguish self-revealed.
I'm naked to the bone,
With nakedness my shield.
Myself is what I wear:
I keep the spirit spare.

The anger will endure,
The deed will speak the truth
In language strict and pure.
I stop the lying mouth:
Rage warps my clearest cry
To witless agony.

FEUD

Corruption reaps the young; you dread
The menace of ancestral eyes;
Recoiling from the serpent head
Of fate, you blubber in surprise.

Exhausted fathers thinned the blood,
You curse the legacy of pain;
Darling of an infected brood,
You feel disaster climb the vein.

There's canker at the root, your seed
Denies the blessing of the sun,
The light essential to your need.
Your hopes are murdered and undone.

The dead leap at the throat, destroy
The meaning of the day; dark forms
Have scaled your walls, and spies betray
Old secrets to amorphous swarms.

You meditate upon the nerves,
Inflame with hate. This ancient feud
Is seldom won. The spirit starves
Until the dead have been subdued.

DEATH PIECE

Invention sleeps within a skull
No longer quick with light,
The hive that hummed in every cell
Is now sealed honey-tight.

His thought is tied, the curving prow
Of motion moored to rock;
And minutes burst upon a brow
Insentient to shock.

PROGNOSIS

Diffuse the outpourings of the spiritual coward,
The rambling lies invented for the sick.
O see the fate of him whose guard was lowered!—
A single misstep and we leave the quick.

Flesh behind steel and glass is unprotected
From enemies that whisper to the blood;
The scratch forgotten is the scratch infected;
The ruminant, reason, chews a poisoned cud.

Platitudes garnished beyond a fool's gainsaying;
The scheme without purpose; pride in a furnished room;
The mediocre busy at betraying
Themselves, their parlors musty as a funeral home.

Though the devouring mother cry, " 'Escape me?
        Never—' "
And the honeymoon be spoiled by a father's ghost,
Chill depths of the spirit are flushed to a fever,
The nightmare silence is broken. We are not lost.

TO MY SISTER

O my sister remember the stars the tears the trains
The woods in spring the leaves the scented lanes
Recall the gradual dark the snow's unmeasured fall
The naked fields the cloud's immaculate folds
Recount each childhood pleasure: the skies of azure
The pageantry of wings the eye's bright treasure.

Keep faith with present joys refuse to choose
Defer the vice of flesh the irrevocable choice
Cherish the eyes the proud incredible poise
Walk boldly my sister but do not deign to give
Remain secure from pain preserve thy hate thy heart.

THE PREMONITION

Walking this field I remember
Days of another summer.
Oh that was long ago! I kept
Close to the heels of my father,
Matching his stride with half-steps
Until we came to a river.
He dipped his hand in the shallow:
Water ran over and under
Hair on a narrow wrist bone;
His image kept following after,—
Flashed with the sun in the ripple.
But when he stood up, that face
Was lost in a maze of water.

INTERLUDE

The element of air was out of hand.
The rush of wind ripped off the tender leaves
And flung them in confusion on the land.
We waited for the first rain in the eaves.

The chaos grew as hour by hour the light
Decreased beneath an undivided sky.
Our pupils widened with unnatural night,
But still the road and dusty field kept dry.

The rain stayed in its cloud; full dark came near;
The wind lay motionless in the long grass.
The veins within our hands betrayed our fear.
What we had hoped for had not come to pass.

6

ORDERS FOR THE DAY

Hands, hard and veined all over,
Perform your duties well,
For carelessness can smother
Decision's smoking fuse;
The flesh-bound sighing lover,
His clumsy fingers bruise
The spirit's tender cover.

Feet, bear the thin bones over
The stile of innocence,
Skirt hatred's raging river,
The dangerous flooded plain
Where snake and vulture hover,
And, stalking like a crane,
Cross marshland into clover.

Eyes, staring past another
Whose bogey-haunted look
Reveals a foolish mother,
Those barriers circumvent
And charity discover
Among the virulent.
Breath, turn the old blood over.

PRAYER

If I must of my Senses lose,
I pray Thee, Lord, that I may choose
Which of the Five I shall retain
Before oblivion clouds the brain.
My Tongue is generations dead,
My Nose defiles a comely head;
For hearkening to carnal evils
My Ears have been the very devil's.
And some have held the Eye to be
The instrument of lechery,
More furtive than the Hand in low
And vicious venery—Not so!
Its rape is gentle, never more
Violent than a metaphor.
In truth, the Eye's the abettor of
The holiest platonic love:
Lip, Breast and Thigh cannot possess
So singular a blessedness.
Therefore, O Lord, let me preserve
The Sense that does so fitly serve,
Take Tongue and Ear—all else I have—
Let Light attend me to the grave!

THE SIGNALS

Often I meet, on walking from a door,
A flash of objects never seen before.

As known particulars come wheeling by,
They dart across a corner of the eye.

They flicker faster than a blue-tailed swift,
Or when dark follows dark in lightning rift.

They slip between the fingers of my sight.
I cannot put my glance upon them tight.

Sometimes the blood is privileged to guess
The things the eye or hand cannot possess.

THE ADAMANT

Thought does not crush to stone.
The great sledge drops in vain.
Truth never is undone;
Its shafts remain.

The teeth of knitted gears
Turn slowly through the night,
But the true substance bears
The hammer's weight.

Compression cannot break
A center so congealed;
The tool can chip no flake:
The core lies sealed.

THE LIGHT COMES BRIGHTER

The light comes brighter from the east; the caw
Of restive crows is sharper on the ear.
A walker at the river's edge may hear
A cannon crack announce an early thaw.

The sun cuts deep into the heavy drift,
Though still the guarded snow is winter-sealed,
At bridgeheads buckled ice begins to shift,
The river overflows the level field.

Once more the trees assume familiar shapes,
As branches loose last vestiges of snow.
The water stored in narrow pools escapes
In rivulets; the cold roots stir below.

Soon field and wood will wear an April look,
The frost be gone, for green is breaking now;
The ovenbird will match the vocal brook,
The young fruit swell upon the pear-tree bough.

And soon a branch, part of a hidden scene,
The leafy mind, that long was tightly furled,
Will turn its private substance into green,
And young shoots spread upon our inner world.

SLOW SEASON

Now light is less; noon skies are wide and deep;
The ravages of wind and rain are healed.
The haze of harvest drifts along the field
Until clear eyes put on the look of sleep.

The garden spider weaves a silken pear
To keep inclement weather from its young.
Straight from the oak, the gossamer is hung.
At dusk our slow breath thickens on the air.

Lost hues of birds the trees take as their own.
Long since, bronze wheat was gathered into sheaves.
The walker trudges ankle-deep in leaves;
The feather of the milkweed flutters down.

The shoots of spring have mellowed with the year.
Buds, long unsealed, obscure the narrow lane.
The blood slows trance-like in the altered vein;
Our vernal wisdom moves through ripe to sere.

MID-COUNTRY BLOW

All night and all day the wind roared in the trees,
Until I could think there were waves rolling high as my bedroom floor;
When I stood at the window, an elm bough swept to my knees;
The blue spruce lashed like a surf at the door.

The second dawn I would not have believed:
The oak stood with each leaf stiff as a bell.
When I looked at the altered scene, my eye was undeceived,
But my ear still kept the sound of the sea like a shell.

IN PRAISE OF PRAIRIE

The elm tree is our highest mountain peak;
A five-foot drop a valley, so to speak.

A man's head is an eminence upon
A field of barley spread beneath the sun.

Horizons have no strangeness to the eye.
Our feet are sometimes level with the sky,

When we are walking on a treeless plain,
With ankles bruised from stubble of the grain.

The fields stretch out in long, unbroken rows.
We walk aware of what is far and close.

Here distance is familiar as a friend.
The feud we kept with space comes to an end.

THE COMING OF THE COLD

1

The late peach yields a subtle musk,
The arbor is alive with fume
More heady than a field at dusk
When clover scents diminished wind.
The walker's foot has scarcely room
Upon the orchard path, for skinned
And battered fruit has choked the grass.
The yield's half down and half in air,
The plum drops pitch upon the ground,
And nostrils widen as they pass
The place where butternuts are found.
The wind shakes out the scent of pear.
Upon the field the scent is dry:
The dill bears up its acrid crown;
The dock, so garish to the eye,
Distills a pungence of its own;
And pumpkins sweat a bitter oil.
But soon cold rain and frost come in
To press pure fragrance to the soil;
The loose vine droops with hoar at dawn,
The riches of the air blow thin.

2

The ribs of leaves lie in the dust,
The beak of frost has picked the bough,
The briar bears its thorn, and drought
Has left its ravage on the field.
The season's wreckage lies about,
Late autumn fruit is rotted now.
All shade is lean, the antic branch
Jerks skyward at the touch of wind,
Dense trees no longer hold the light,
The hedge and orchard grove are thinned.
The dank bark dries beneath the sun,
The last of harvesting is done.
All things are brought to barn and fold.

The oak leaves strain to be unbound,
The sky turns dark, the year grows old,
The buds draw in before the cold.

3

The small brook dies within its bed;
The stem that holds the bee is prone;
Old hedgerows keep the leaves; the phlox,
That late autumnal bloom, is dead.
All summer green is now undone:
The hills are grey, the trees are bare,
The mould upon the branch is dry,
The fields are harsh and bare, the rocks
Gleam sharply on the narrow sight.
The land is desolate, the sun
No longer gilds the scene at noon;
Winds gather in the north and blow
Bleak clouds across the heavy sky,
And frost is marrow-cold, and soon
Winds bring a fine and bitter snow.

THE HERON

The heron stands in water where the swamp
Has deepened to the blackness of a pool,
Or balances with one leg on a hump
Of marsh grass heaped above a musk-rat hole.

He walks the shallow with an antic grace.
The great feet break the ridges of the sand,
The long eye notes the minnow's hiding place.
His beak is quicker than a human hand.

He jerks a frog across his bony lip,
Then points his heavy bill above the wood.
The wide wings flap but once to lift him up.
A single ripple starts from where he stood.

THE BAT

By day the bat is cousin to the mouse.
He likes the attic of an aging house.

His fingers make a hat about his head.
His pulse beat is so slow we think him dead.

He loops in crazy figures half the night
Among the trees that face the corner light.

But when he brushes up against a screen,
We are afraid of what our eyes have seen:

For something is amiss or out of place
When mice with wings can wear a human face.

III

NO BIRD

       Now here is peace for one who knew
       The secret heart of sound.
       The ear so delicate and true
       Is pressed to noiseless ground.

       Slow swings the breeze above her head,
       The grasses whitely stir;
       But in this forest of the dead
       No bird awakens her.

THE UNEXTINGUISHED

       Clouds glow like coals just fresh from fire, a flare
       Of western light leaps with intenser blaze
       To conflagration in the upper air.
       All distant shapes turn brighter to the gaze.

       The fire of heaven dies; a fire unseen
       Wanes to the febrile smoldering of sleep;
       Deep-hidden embers, smothered by the screen
       Of flesh, burn backward to a blackened heap.

       But morning light comes tapping at the lid,
       Breaks up the crust of cinders that remain,
       And pokes the crumbled coal the ashes hid,
       Until thought crackles white across the brain.

"LONG LIVE THE WEEDS"
Hopkins

Long live the weeds that overwhelm
My narrow vegetable realm!
The bitter rock, the barren soil
That force the son of man to toil;
All things unholy, marred by curse,
The ugly of the universe.
The rough, the wicked, and the wild
That keep the spirit undefiled.
With these I match my little wit
And earn the right to stand or sit,
Hope, love, create, or drink and die:
These shape the creature that is I.

GENESIS

This elemental force
Was wrested from the sun;
A river's leaping source
Is locked in narrow bone.

This wisdom floods the mind,
Invades quiescent blood;
A seed that swells the rind
To burst the fruit of good.

A pearl within the brain,
Secretion of the sense;
Around a central grain
New meaning grows immense.

17

EPIDERMAL MACABRE

Indelicate is he who loathes
The aspect of his fleshy clothes,—
The flying fabric stitched on bone,
The vesture of the skeleton,
The garment neither fur nor hair,
The cloak of evil and despair,
The veil long violated by
Caresses of the hand and eye.
Yet such is my unseemliness:
I hate my epidermal dress,
The savage blood's obscenity,
The rags of my anatomy,
And willingly would I dispense
With false accouterments of sense,
To sleep immodestly, a most
Incarnadine and carnal ghost.

AGAINST DISASTER

Now I am out of element
And far from anything my own,
My sources drained of all content,
The pieces of my spirit strewn.

All random, wasted, and dispersed,
The particles of being lie;
My special heaven is reversed,
I move beneath an evil sky.

This flat land has become a pit
Wherein I am beset by harm,
The heart must rally to my wit
And rout the specter of alarm.

REPLY TO CENSURE

Repulse the staring eye,
The hostile gaze of hate,
And check the pedantry
Of those inveterate

Defamers of the good.
They mock the deepest thought,
Condemn the fortitude
Whereby true work is wrought.

Though just men are reviled
When cravens cry them down,
The brave keep undefiled
A wisdom of their own.

The bold wear toughened skin
That keeps sufficient store
Of dignity within,
And quiet at the core.

THE AUCTION

Once on returning home, purse-proud and hale,
I found my choice possessions on the lawn.
An auctioneer was whipping up a sale.
I did not move to claim what was my own.

"One coat of pride, perhaps a bit threadbare;
Illusion's trinkets, splendid for the young;
Some items, miscellaneous, marked 'Fear';
The chair of honor, with a missing rung."

The spiel ran on; the sale was brief and brisk;
The bargains fell to bidders, one by one.
Hope flushed my cheekbones with a scarlet disk.
Old neighbors nudged each other at the fun.

My spirits rose each time the hammer fell,
The heart beat faster as the fat words rolled.
I left my home with unencumbered will
And all the rubbish of confusion sold.

SILENCE

There is a noise within the brow
That pulses undiminished now
In accents measured by the blood.
It breaks upon my solitude—
A hammer on the crystal walls
Of sense at rapid intervals.
It is the unmelodic ring
Before the breaking of a string,
The wheels of circumstance that grind
So terribly within the mind,
The spirit crying in a cage
To build a complement to rage,
Confusion's core set deep within
A furious, dissembling din.

If I should ever seek relief
From that monotony of grief,
The tight nerves leading to the throat
Would not release one riven note:
What shakes my skull to disrepair
Shall never touch another ear.

ON THE ROAD TO WOODLAWN

I miss the polished brass, the powerful black horses,
The drivers creaking the seats of the baroque hearses,
The high-piled floral offerings with sentimental verses,
The carriages reeking with varnish and stale perfume.

I miss the pallbearers momentously taking their places,
The undertaker's obsequious grimaces,
The craned necks, the mourners' anonymous faces,
—And the eyes, still vivid, looking up from a sunken room.

21

IV

ACADEMIC

The stethoscope tells what everyone fears:
You're likely to go on living for years,
With a nurse-maid waddle and a shop-girl simper,
And the style of your prose growing limper and limper.

FOR AN AMOROUS LADY

> *"Most mammals like caresses, in the sense in which*
> *we usually take the word, whereas other creatures,*
> *even tame snakes, prefer giving to receiving them."*
> FROM A NATURAL-HISTORY BOOK

The pensive gnu, the staid aardvark,
Accept caresses in the dark;
The bear, equipped with paw and snout;
Would rather take than dish it out.
But snakes, both poisonous and garter,
In love are never known to barter;
The worm, though dank, is sensitive:
His noble nature bids him *give*.

But you, my dearest, have a soul
Encompassing fish, flesh, and fowl.
When amorous arts we would pursue,
You can, with pleasure, bill *or* coo.
You are, in truth, one in a million,
At once mammalian and reptilian.

POETASTER

Hero of phantasies and catcher of chills,
Wants singleness of spirit above all else:
Happy alone in his bedroom counting his pulse.
O fortunate he whose mamma pays the bills!

VERNAL SENTIMENT

Though the crocuses poke up their heads in the usual places,
The frog scum appear on the pond with the same froth of green,
And boys moon at girls with last year's fatuous faces,
I never am bored, however familiar the scene.

When from under the barn the cat brings a similar litter,—
Two yellow and black, and one that looks in between,—
Though it all happened before, I cannot grow bitter:
I rejoice in the spring, as though no spring ever had been.

PRAYER BEFORE STUDY

Constricted by my tortured thought,
I am too centred on this spot.

So caged and cadged, so close within
A coat of unessential skin,

I would put off myself and flee
My inaccessibility.

A fool can play at being solemn
Revolving on his spinal column.

Deliver me, O Lord, from all
Activity centripetal.

MY DIM-WIT COUSIN

My dim-wit cousin, saved by a death-bed quaver,
Your little manhood long ago was smothered.
But for an uncle you were thought to favor,
Those doting aunties never would have bothered.

The cost of folly is forever mounting;
Your bed collapses from imagined sins.
Deterioration's scrupulous accounting
Adds up a pair of jiggling double chins.

Your palm is moist, your manner far too jolly . . .
Today, while scraping hair before the mirror,
My shaving hand jerked back in sudden terror:
I heard your laughter rumble from my belly.

VERSE WITH ALLUSIONS

Thrice happy they whose world is spanned
By the circumference of Hand,

Who want no more than Fingers seize,
And scorn the Abstract Entities.

The Higher Things in Life do not
Invade their privacy of Thought.

Their only notion of the Good
Is Human Nature's Daily Food.

They feed the Sense, deny the Soul,
But view things steadily and whole.

I, starveling yearner, seem to see
Much logic in their Gluttony.

V

BALLAD OF THE CLAIRVOYANT WIDOW

A kindly Widow Lady, who lived upon a hill,
Climbed to her attic window and gazed across the sill.

"Oh tell me, Widow Lady, what is it that you see,
   As you look across my city, in God's country?"

"I see ten million windows, I see ten thousand streets,
I see the traffic doing miraculous feats.

The lawyers all are cunning, the business men are fat,
Their wives go out on Sunday beneath the latest hat.

The kids play cops and robbers, the kids play mumbley-peg,
Some learn the art of thieving, and some grow up to beg;

The rich can play at polo, the poor can do the shag,
Professors are condoning the cultural lag.

I see a banker's mansion with twenty wood-grate fires,
Alone, his wife is grieving for what her heart desires.

Next door there is a love-nest of plaster board and tin,
The rats soon will be leaving, the snow will come in."

"Clairvoyant Widow Lady, with an eye like a telescope,
   Do you see any sign or semblance of that thing called 'Hope'?"

"I see the river harbor, alive with men and ships,
A surgeon guides a scalpel with thumb and finger-tips.

I see grandpa surviving a series of seven strokes,
The unemployed are telling stale unemployment jokes.

The gulls ride on the water, the gulls have come and gone,
The men on rail and roadway keep moving on and on.

The salmon climb the rivers, the rivers nudge the sea,
The green comes up forever in the fields of our country."

THE FAVORITE

A knave who scampered through the needle's eye,
He never trembled at a veiled remark.
His oyster world was easily come by;
There were no nights of sleeping in the park.

Fearless and bold, he did his fellows in,
Only to gain fresh triumphs and applause.
His insolence could wear no patience thin.
He lived beyond the touch of mortal laws.

O he was Fortune's child, a favorite son
Upon whom every gift and thrill were showered,
And yet his happiness was not complete;
Slowly his matchless disposition soured
Until he cried at enemies undone
And longed to feel the impact of defeat.

THE REMINDER

I remember the crossing-tender's geranium border
That blossomed in soot; a black cat licking its paw;
The bronze wheat arranged in strict and formal order;
And the precision that for you was ultimate law:

The handkerchief tucked in the left-hand pocket
Of a man-tailored blouse; the list of shopping done;
You wound the watch in an old-fashioned locket
And pulled the green shade against morning sun.

Now in the misery of bed-sitting room confusion,
With no hint of your presence in a jungle of masculine toys,
In the dirt and disorder I cherish one scrap of illusion:
A cheap clock ticking in ghostly cicada voice.

THE GENTLE

Delicate the syllables that release the repression;
Hysteria masks in the studied inane.
Horace the hiker on a dubious mission
Pretends his dead bunion gives exquisite pain.

The son of misfortune long, long has been waiting
The visit of vision, luck years overdue,
His laughter reduced the sing-song of prating,
A hutch by the EXIT his room with a view.

O cursed be the work that gets honorable mention!
Though home is not happy, where else can he go?
Necessity starves on the stoop of invention.
The sleep was not deep, but the waking is slow.

THE RECKONING

All profits disappear: the gain
Of ease, the hoarded, secret sum;
And now grim digits of old pain
Return to litter up our home.

We hunt the cause of ruin, add,
Subtract, and put ourselves in pawn;
For all our scratching on the pad,
We cannot trace the error down.

What we are seeking is a fare
One way, a chance to be secure:
The lack that keeps us what we are,
The penny that usurps the poor.

LULL
(November, 1939)

The winds of hatred blow
Cold, cold across the flesh,
And chill the anxious heart;
Intricate phobias grow
From each malignant wish
To spoil collective life.
Now each man stands apart.

We watch opinion drift,
Think of our separate skins.
On well-upholstered bums
The generals cough and shift
Playing with painted pins.
The arbitrators wait;
The newsmen suck their thumbs.
The mind is quick to turn
Away from simple faith
To the cant and fury of
Fools who will never learn;
Reason embraces death,
While out of frightened eyes
Still stares the wish to love.

SALE

For sale: by order of the remaining heirs
Who ran up and down the big center stairs
The what-not, the settee, the Chippendale chairs
—And an attic of horrors, a closet of fears.

The furniture polished and polished so grand,
A stable and paddock, some fox-hunting land,
The summer house shaped like a village band stand
—And grandfather's sinister hovering hand.

The antimacassar for the sofa in red,
The Bechstein piano, the four-poster bed,
The library used as a card room instead
—And some watery eyes in a Copley head.

The dining room carpet dyed brighter than blood,
The table where everyone ate as he should,
The sideboard beside which a tall footman stood
—And a fume of decay that clings fast to the wood.

The hand-painted wall-paper, finer than skin,
The room that the children had never been in,
All the rings and the relics encrusted with sin
—And the taint in a blood that was running too thin.

HIGHWAY: MICHIGAN

Here from the field's edge we survey
The progress of the jaded. Mile
On mile of traffic from the town
Rides by, for at the end of day
The time of workers is their own.

They jockey for position on
The strip reserved for passing only.
The drivers from production lines
Hold to advantage dearly won.
They toy with death and traffic fines.

Acceleration is their need:
A mania keeps them on the move
Until the toughest nerves are frayed.
They are the prisoners of speed
Who flee in what their hands have made.

The pavement smokes when two cars meet
And steel rips through conflicting steel.
We shiver at the siren's blast.
One driver, pinned beneath the seat,
Escapes from the machine at last.

IDYLL

Now as from maple to elm the flittermice skitter and twirl,
A drunk man stumbles by, absorbed in self-talk.
The lights in the kitchens go out; moth wings unfurl;
The last tricycle runs crazily to the end of the walk.

As darkness creeps up on the well-groomed suburban town,
We grow indifferent to dog howls, to the nestling's last peep;
Dew deepens on the fresh-cut lawn;
We sit in the porch swing, content and half asleep.

The world recedes in the black revolving shadow;
A far-off train blows its echoing whistle once;
We go to our beds in a house at the edge of a meadow,
Unmindful of terror and headlines, of speeches and guns.

NIGHT JOURNEY

Now as the train bears west,
Its rhythm rocks the earth,
And from my Pullman berth
I stare into the night
While others take their rest.
Bridges of iron lace,
A suddenness of trees,
A lap of mountain mist
All cross my line of sight,
Then a bleak wasted place,
And a lake below my knees.
Full on my neck I feel
The straining at a curve;
My muscles move with steel,
I wake in every nerve.
I watch a beacon swing
From dark to blazing bright;
We thunder through ravines
And gullies washed with light.
Beyond the mountain pass
Mist deepens on the pane;
We rush into a rain
That rattles double glass.
Wheels shake the roadbed stone,
The pistons jerk and shove,
I stay up half the night
To see the land I love.

THE LOST SON AND OTHER POEMS

1948

I

CUTTINGS

Sticks-in-a-drowse droop over sugary loam,
Their intricate stem-fur dries;
But still the delicate slips keep coaxing up water;
The small cells bulge;

One nub of growth
Nudges a sand-crumb loose,
Pokes through a musty sheath
Its pale tendrilous horn.

CUTTINGS
(*later*)

This urge, wrestle, resurrection of dry sticks,
Cut stems struggling to put down feet,
What saint strained so much,
Rose on such lopped limbs to a new life?

I can hear, underground, that sucking and sobbing,
In my veins, in my bones I feel it,—
The small waters seeping upward,
The tight grains parting at last.
When sprouts break out,
Slippery as fish,
I quail, lean to beginnings, sheath-wet.

ROOT CELLAR

Nothing would sleep in that cellar, dank as a ditch,
Bulbs broke out of boxes hunting for chinks in the dark,
Shoots dangled and drooped,
Lolling obscenely from mildewed crates,
Hung down long yellow evil necks, like tropical snakes.
And what a congress of stinks!—
Roots ripe as old bait,
Pulpy stems, rank, silo-rich,
Leaf-mold, manure, lime, piled against slippery planks.
Nothing would give up life:
Even the dirt kept breathing a small breath.

FORCING HOUSE

Vines tougher than wrists
And rubbery shoots,
Scums, mildews, smuts along stems,
Great cannas or delicate cyclamen tips,—
All pulse with the knocking pipes
That drip and sweat,
Sweat and drip,
Swelling the roots with steam and stench,
Shooting up lime and dung and ground bones,—
Fifty summers in motion at once,
As the live heat billows from pipes and pots.

WEED PULLER

Under the concrete benches,
Hacking at black hairy roots,—
Those lewd monkey-tails hanging from drainholes,—
Digging into the soft rubble underneath,
Webs and weeds,
Grubs and snails and sharp sticks,
Or yanking tough fern-shapes,
Coiled green and thick, like dripping smilax,
Tugging all day at perverse life:
The indignity of it!—
With everything blooming above me,
Lilies, pale-pink cyclamen, roses,
Whole fields lovely and inviolate,—
Me down in that fetor of weeds,
Crawling on all fours,
Alive, in a slippery grave.

ORCHIDS

They lean over the path,
Adder-mouthed,
Swaying close to the face,
Coming out, soft and deceptive,
Limp and damp, delicate as a young bird's tongue;
Their fluttery fledgling lips
Move slowly,
Drawing in the warm air.

And at night,
The faint moon falling through whitewashed glass,
The heat going down
So their musky smell comes even stronger,
Drifting down from their mossy cradles:
So many devouring infants!
Soft luminescent fingers,
Lips neither dead nor alive,
Loose ghostly mouths
Breathing.

MOSS-GATHERING

To loosen with all ten fingers held wide and limber
And lift up a patch, dark-green, the kind for lining cemetery baskets,
Thick and cushiony, like an old-fashioned doormat,
The crumbling small hollow sticks on the underside mixed with roots,
And wintergreen berries and leaves still stuck to the top,—
That was moss-gathering.
But something always went out of me when I dug loose those carpets
Of green, or plunged to my elbows in the spongy yellowish moss of the
        marshes:
And afterwards I always felt mean, jogging back over the logging road,
As if I had broken the natural order of things in that swampland;
Disturbed some rhythm, old and of vast importance,
By pulling off flesh from the living planet;
As if I had committed, against the whole scheme of life, a desecration.

BIG WIND

Where were the greenhouses going,
Lunging into the lashing
Wind driving water
So far down the river
All the faucets stopped?—
So we drained the manure-machine
For the steam plant,
Pumping the stale mixture
Into the rusty boilers,
Watching the pressure gauge
Waver over to red,
As the seams hissed
And the live steam
Drove to the far
End of the rose-house,
Where the worst wind was,
Creaking the cypress window-frames,
Cracking so much thin glass
We stayed all night,
Stuffing the holes with burlap;
But she rode it out,
That old rose-house,
She hove into the teeth of it,
The core and pith of that ugly storm,
Ploughing with her stiff prow,
Bucking into the wind-waves
That broke over the whole of her,
Flailing her sides with spray,
Flinging long strings of wet across the roof-top,
Finally veering, wearing themselves out, merely
Whistling thinly under the wind-vents;
She sailed until the calm morning,
Carrying her full cargo of roses.

OLD FLORIST

That hump of a man bunching chrysanthemums
Or pinching-back asters, or planting azaleas,
Tamping and stamping dirt into pots,—
How he could flick and pick
Rotten leaves or yellowy petals,
Or scoop out a weed close to flourishing roots,
Or make the dust buzz with a light spray,
Or drown a bug in one spit of tobacco juice,
Or fan life into wilted sweet-peas with his hat,
Or stand all night watering roses, his feet blue in rubber boots.

TRANSPLANTING

Watching hands transplanting,
Turning and tamping,
Lifting the young plants with two fingers,
Sifting in a palm-full of fresh loam,—
One swift movement,—
Then plumping in the bunched roots,
A single twist of the thumbs, a tamping and turning,
All in one,
Quick on the wooden bench,
A shaking down, while the stem stays straight,
Once, twice, and a faint third thump,—
Into the flat-box it goes,
Ready for the long days under the sloped glass:

The sun warming the fine loam,
The young horns winding and unwinding,
Creaking their thin spines,
The underleaves, the smallest buds
Breaking into nakedness,
The blossoms extending
Out into the sweet air,
The whole flower extending outward,
Stretching and reaching.

CHILD ON TOP OF A GREENHOUSE

The wind billowing out the seat of my britches,
My feet crackling splinters of glass and dried putty,
The half-grown chrysanthemums staring up like accusers,
Up through the streaked glass, flashing with sunlight,
A few white clouds all rushing eastward,
A line of elms plunging and tossing like horses,
And everyone, everyone pointing up and shouting!

FLOWER DUMP

Cannas shiny as slag,
Slug-soft stems,
Whole beds of bloom pitched on a pile,
Carnations, verbenas, cosmos,
Molds, weeds, dead leaves,
Turned-over roots
With bleached veins
Twined like fine hair,
Each clump in the shape of a pot;
Everything limp
But one tulip on top,
One swaggering head
Over the dying, the newly dead.

CARNATIONS

Pale blossoms, each balanced on a single jointed stem,
The leaves curled back in elaborate Corinthian scrolls;
And the air cool, as if drifting down from wet hemlocks,
Or rising out of ferns not far from water,
A crisp hyacinthine coolness,
Like that clear autumnal weather of eternity,
The windless perpetual morning above a September cloud.

FRAU BAUMAN, FRAU SCHMIDT, AND
FRAU SCHWARTZE

Gone the three ancient ladies
Who creaked on the greenhouse ladders,
Reaching up white strings
To wind, to wind
The sweet-pea tendrils, the smilax,
Nasturtiums, the climbing
Roses, to straighten
Carnations, red
Chrysanthemums; the stiff
Stems, jointed like corn,
They tied and tucked,—
These nurses of nobody else.
Quicker than birds, they dipped
Up and sifted the dirt;
They sprinkled and shook;
They stood astride pipes,
Their skirts billowing out wide into tents,
Their hands twinkling with wet;
Like witches they flew along rows
Keeping creation at ease;
With a tendril for needle
They sewed up the air with a stem;
They teased out the seed that the cold kept asleep,—
All the coils, loops, and whorls.
They trellised the sun; they plotted for more than themselves.

I remember how they picked me up, a spindly kid,
Pinching and poking my thin ribs
Till I lay in their laps, laughing,
Weak as a whiffet;
Now, when I'm alone and cold in my bed,
They still hover over me,
These ancient leathery crones,
With their bandannas stiffened with sweat,
And their thorn-bitten wrists,
And their snuff-laden breath blowing lightly over me in my first sleep.

II

MY PAPA'S WALTZ

The whiskey on your breath
Could make a small boy dizzy;
But I hung on like death:
Such waltzing was not easy.

We romped until the pans
Slid from the kitchen shelf;
My mother's countenance
Could not unfrown itself.

The hand that held my wrist
Was battered on one knuckle;
At every step you missed
My right ear scraped a buckle.

You beat time on my head
With a palm caked hard by dirt,
Then waltzed me off to bed
Still clinging to your shirt.

PICKLE BELT

The fruit rolled by all day.
They prayed the cogs would creep;
They thought about Saturday pay,
And Sunday sleep.

Whatever he smelled was good:
The fruit and flesh smells mixed.
There beside him she stood,—
And he, perplexed;

He, in his shrunken britches,
Eyes rimmed with pickle dust,
Prickling with all the itches
Of sixteen-year-old lust.

DOLOR

I have known the inexorable sadness of pencils,
Neat in their boxes, dolor of pad and paper-weight,
All the misery of manilla folders and mucilage,
Desolation in immaculate public places,
Lonely reception room, lavatory, switchboard,
The unalterable pathos of basin and pitcher,
Ritual of multigraph, paper-clip, comma,
Endless duplication of lives and objects.
And I have seen dust from the walls of institutions,
Finer than flour, alive, more dangerous than silica,
Sift, almost invisible, through long afternoons of tedium,
Dropping a fine film on nails and delicate eyebrows,
Glazing the pale hair, the duplicate grey standard faces.

DOUBLE FEATURE

With Buck still tied to the log, on comes the light.
Lovers disengage, move sheepishly toward the aisle
With mothers, sleep-heavy children, stale perfume, past the manager's
    smile
Out through the velvety chains to the cool air of night.

I dawdle with groups near the rickety pop-corn stand;
Dally at shop windows, still reluctant to go;
I teeter, heels hooked on the curb, scrape a toe;
Or send off a car with vague lifts of a hand.

A wave of Time hangs motionless on this particular shore.
I notice a tree, arsenical grey in the light, or the slow
Wheel of the stars, the Great Bear glittering colder than snow,
And remember there was something else I was hoping for.

THE RETURN

       I circled on leather paws
       In the darkening corridor,
       Crouched closer to the floor,
       Then bristled like a dog.

       As I turned for a backward look,
       The muscles in one thigh
       Sagged like a frightened lip.

       A cold key let me in
       That self-infected lair;
       And I lay down with my life,
       With the rags and rotting clothes,
       With a stump of scraggy fang
       Bared for a hunter's boot.

LAST WORDS

Solace of kisses and cookies and cabbage,
That fine fuming stink of particular kettles,
Muttony tears falling on figured linoleum,
Frigidaires snoring the sleep of plenty,
The psyche writhing and squirming in heavy woolen,—
O worm of duty! O spiral knowledge!

Kiss me, kiss me quick, mistress of lost wisdom,
Come out of a cloud, angel with several faces,
Bring me my hat, my umbrella and rubbers,
Enshroud me with Light! O Whirling! O Terrible Love!

JUDGE NOT

Faces greying faster than loam-crumbs on a harrow;
Children, their bellies swollen like blown-up paper bags,
Their eyes, rich as plums, staring from newsprint,—
These images haunted me noon and midnight.
I imagined the unborn, starving in wombs, curling;
I asked: May the blessings of life, O Lord, descend on the living.

Yet when I heard the drunkards howling,
Smelled the carrion at entrances,
Saw women, their eyelids like little rags,
I said: On all these, Death, with gentleness, come down.

III

NIGHT CROW

When I saw that clumsy crow
Flap from a wasted tree,
A shape in the mind rose up:
Over the gulfs of dream
Flew a tremendous bird
Further and further away
Into a moonless black,
Deep in the brain, far back.

RIVER INCIDENT

A shell arched under my toes,
Stirred up a whirl of silt
That riffled around my knees.
Whatever I owed to time
Slowed in my human form;
Sea water stood in my veins,
The elements I kept warm
Crumbled and flowed away,
And I knew I had been there before,
In that cold, granitic slime,
In the dark, in the rolling water.

THE MINIMAL

I study the lives on a leaf: the little
Sleepers, numb nudgers in cold dimensions,
Beetles in caves, newts, stone-deaf fishes,
Lice tethered to long limp subterranean weeds,
Squirmers in bogs,
And bacterial creepers
Wriggling through wounds
Like elvers in ponds,
Their wan mouths kissing the warm sutures,
Cleaning and caressing,
Creeping and healing.

THE CYCLE

Dark water, underground,
Beneath the rock and clay,
Beneath the roots of trees,
Moved into common day,
Rose from a mossy mound
In mist that sun could seize.

The fine rain coiled in a cloud
Turned by revolving air
Far from that colder source
Where elements cohere
Dense in the central stone.
The air grew loose and loud.

Then, with diminished force,
The full rain fell straight down,
Tunneled with lapsing sound
Under even the rock-shut ground,
Under a river's source,
Under primeval stone.

48

THE WAKING

I strolled across
An open field;
The sun was out;
Heat was happy.

This way! This way!
The wren's throat shimmered,
Either to other,
The blossoms sang.

The stones sang,
The little ones did,
And flowers jumped
Like small goats.

A ragged fringe
Of daisies waved;
I wasn't alone
In a grove of apples.

Far in the wood
A nestling sighed;
The dew loosened
Its morning smells.

I came where the river
Ran over stones:
My ears knew
An early joy.

And all the waters
Of all the streams
Sang in my veins
That summer day.

IV

THE LOST SON

1. *The Flight*

At Woodlawn I heard the dead cry:
I was lulled by the slamming of iron,
A slow drip over stones,
Toads brooding wells.
All the leaves stuck out their tongues;
I shook the softening chalk of my bones,
Saying,
Snail, snail, glister me forward,
Bird, soft-sigh me home,
Worm, be with me.
This is my hard time.

Fished in an old wound,
The soft pond of repose;
Nothing nibbled my line,
Not even the minnows came.

Sat in an empty house
Watching shadows crawl,
Scratching.
There was one fly.

Voice, come out of the silence.
Say something.
Appear in the form of a spider
Or a moth beating the curtain.

Tell me:
Which is the way I take;
Out of what door do I go,
Where and to whom?

     Dark hollows said, lee to the wind,
     The moon said, back of an eel,
     The salt said, look by the sea,
     Your tears are not enough praise,
     You will find no comfort here,
     In the kingdom of bang and blab.

     Running lightly over spongy ground,
     Past the pasture of flat stones,
     The three elms,
     The sheep strewn on a field,
     Over a rickety bridge
     Toward the quick-water, wrinkling and rippling.

     Hunting along the river,
     Down among the rubbish, the bug-riddled foliage,
     By the muddy pond-edge, by the bog-holes,
     By the shrunken lake, hunting, in the heat of summer.

The shape of a rat?
     It's bigger than that.
     It's less than a leg
     And more than a nose,
     Just under the water
     It usually goes.

     Is it soft like a mouse?
     Can it wrinkle its nose?
     Could it come in the house
     On the tips of its toes?

Take the skin of a cat
And the back of an eel,
Then roll them in grease,—
That's the way it would feel.

It's sleek as an otter
With wide webby toes
Just under the water
It usually goes.

2. The Pit

Where do the roots go?
    Look down under the leaves.
Who put the moss there?
    These stones have been here too long.
Who stunned the dirt into noise?
    Ask the mole, he knows.
I feel the slime of a wet nest.
    Beware Mother Mildew.
Nibble again, fish nerves.

3. The Gibber

At the wood's mouth,
By the cave's door,
I listened to something
I had heard before.

Dogs of the groin
Barked and howled,
The sun was against me,
The moon would not have me.

The weeds whined,
The snakes cried,
The cows and briars
Said to me: Die.

What a small song. What slow clouds. What dark water.
Hath the rain a father? All the caves are ice. Only the snow's here.
I'm cold. I'm cold all over. Rub me in father and mother.
Fear was my father, Father Fear.
His look drained the stones.

What gliding shape
Beckoning through halls,
Stood poised on the stair,
Fell dreamily down?

From the mouths of jugs
Perched on many shelves,
I saw substance flowing
That cold morning.

Like a slither of eels
That watery cheek
As my own tongue kissed
My lips awake.

Is this the storm's heart? The ground is unstilling itself.
My veins are running nowhere. Do the bones cast out their fire?
Is the seed leaving the old bed? These buds are live as birds.
Where, where are the tears of the world?
Let the kisses resound, flat like a butcher's palm;
Let the gestures freeze; our doom is already decided.
All the windows are burning! What's left of my life?
I want the old rage, the lash of primordial milk!
Goodbye, goodbye, old stones, the time-order is going,
I have married my hands to perpetual agitation,
I run, I run to the whistle of money.

Money money money
Water water water

How cool the grass is.
Has the bird left?
The stalk still sways.
Has the worm a shadow?
What do the clouds say?

53

These sweeps of light undo me.
Look, look, the ditch is running white!
I've more veins than a tree!
Kiss me, ashes, I'm falling through a dark swirl.

4. *The Return*

The way to the boiler was dark,
Dark all the way,
Over slippery cinders
Through the long greenhouse.

The roses kept breathing in the dark.
They had many mouths to breathe with.
My knees made little winds underneath
Where the weeds slept.

There was always a single light
Swinging by the fire-pit,
Where the fireman pulled out roses,
The big roses, the big bloody clinkers.

Once I stayed all night.
The light in the morning came slowly over the white
Snow.
There were many kinds of cool
Air.
Then came steam.

Pipe-knock.

Scurry of warm over small plants.
Ordnung! ordnung!
Papa is coming!

A fine haze moved off the leaves;
Frost melted on far panes;
The rose, the chrysanthemum turned toward the light.
Even the hushed forms, the bent yellowy weeds
Moved in a slow up-sway.

5. *"It was beginning winter"*

It was beginning winter,
An in-between time,
The landscape still partly brown:
The bones of weeds kept swinging in the wind,
Above the blue snow.

It was beginning winter,
The light moved slowly over the frozen field,
Over the dry seed-crowns,
The beautiful surviving bones
Swinging in the wind.

Light traveled over the wide field;
Stayed.
The weeds stopped swinging.
The mind moved, not alone,
Through the clear air, in the silence.

     Was it light?
     Was it light within?
     Was it light within light?
     Stillness becoming alive,
     Yet still?

A lively understandable spirit
Once entertained you.
It will come again.
Be still.
Wait.

THE LONG ALLEY

1

A river glides out of the grass. A river or a serpent.
A fish floats belly upward,
Sliding through the white current,
Slowly turning,
Slowly.

The dark flows on itself. A dead mouth sings under an old tree.
The ear hears only in low places.
Remember an old sound.
Remember
Water.

This slag runs slow. What bleeds when metal breaks?
Flesh, you offend this metal. How long need the bones mourn?
Are those horns on top of the hill? Yesterday has a long look.

Loo, loo, said the sulphurous water,
There's no filth on a plateau of cinders.
This smoke's from the glory of God.

> Can you name it? I can't name it.
> Let's not hurry. The dead don't hurry.
> Who else breathes here? What does the grave say?
> My gates are all caves.

2

The fiend's far away. Lord, what do you require?
> The soul resides in the horse barn.
Believe me, there's no one else, kitten-limp sister.
> Kiss the trough, swine-on-Friday.
Come to me, milk-nose. I need a loan of the quick.
> There's no joy in soft bones.
For whom were you made, sweetness I cannot touch?
> Look what the larks do.
Luminous one, shall we meet on the bosom of God?
> Return the gaze of a pond.

56

3

Stay close. Must I kill something else?
Can feathers eat me? There's no clue in the silt.
This wind gives me scales. Have mercy, gristle:
It's my last waltz with an old itch.

A waiting ghost warms up the dead
Until they creak their knees:
So up and away and what do we do
But barley-break and squeeze.

Tricksy comes and tricksy goes
Bold in fear therefore;
The hay hops in the horse's mouth,
The chin jumps to the nose.

Rich me cherries a fondling's kiss,
The summer bumps of ha:
Hand me a feather, I'll fan you warm,
I'm happy with my paws.

Gilliflower ha,
Gilliflower ho,
My love's locked in
The old silo.

She cries to the hen,
She waves to the goose,
But they don't come
To let her loose.

If we detach
The head of a match
What do we do
To the cat's wish?
Do we rout the fish?
Will the goat's mouth
Have the last laugh?

4

That was a close knock. See what the will wants.
This air could flesh a dead stick. Sweet Jesus, make me sweat.
Are the flowers here? The birds are.
Shall I call the flowers?

    Come littlest, come tenderest,
    Come whispering over the small waters,
    Reach me rose, sweet one, still moist in the loam,
    Come, come out of the shade, the cool ways,
    The long alleys of string and stem;
    Bend down, small breathers, creepers and winders;
    Lean from the tiers and benches,
    Cyclamen dripping and lilies.
    What fish-ways you have, littlest flowers,
    Swaying over the walks, in the watery air,
    Drowsing in soft light, petals pulsing.

Light airs! Light airs! A pierce of angels!
The leaves, the leaves become me!
The tendrils have me!

5

Bricks flake before my face. Master of water, that's trees away.
Reach me a peach, fondling, the hills are there.
Nuts are money: wherefore and what else?
Send down a rush of air, O torrential,
Make the sea flash in the dust.

Call off the dogs, my paws are gone.
This wind brings many fish;
The lakes will be happy:
Give me my hands:
I'll take the fire.

58

A FIELD OF LIGHT

1

Came to lakes; came to dead water,
Ponds with moss and leaves floating,
Planks sunk in the sand.

A log turned at the touch of a foot;
A long weed floated upward;
An eye tilted.

    Small winds made
    A chilly noise;
    The softest cove
    Cried for sound.

    Reached for a grape
    And the leaves changed;
    A stone's shape
    Became a clam.

    A fine rain fell
    On fat leaves;
    I was there alone
    In a watery drowse.

2

Angel within me, I asked,
Did I ever curse the sun?
Speak and abide.

    Under, under the sheaves,
    Under the blackened leaves,
    Behind the green viscid trellis,
    In the deep grass at the edge of field,
    Along the low ground dry only in August,—

Was it dust I was kissing?
A sigh came far.
Alone, I kissed the skin of a stone;
Marrow-soft, danced in the sand.

3

The dirt left my hand, visitor.
I could feel the mare's nose.
A path went walking.
The sun glittered on a small rapids.
Some morning thing came, beating its wings.
The great elm filled with birds.

Listen, love,
The fat lark sang in the field;
I touched the ground, the ground warmed by the killdeer,
The salt laughed and the stones;
The ferns had their ways, and the pulsing lizards,
And the new plants, still awkward in their soil,
The lovely diminutives.
I could watch! I could watch!
I saw the separateness of all things!
My heart lifted up with the great grasses;
The weeds believed me, and the nesting birds.
There were clouds making a rout of shapes crossing a windbreak
    of cedars,
And a bee shaking drops from a rain-soaked honeysuckle.
The worms were delighted as wrens.
And I walked, I walked through the light air;
I moved with the morning.

THE SHAPE OF THE FIRE

1

What's this? A dish for fat lips.
Who says? A nameless stranger.
Is he a bird or a tree? Not everyone can tell.

Water recedes to the crying of spiders.
An old scow bumps over black rocks.
A cracked pod calls.

Mother me out of here. What more will the bones allow?
Will the sea give the wind suck? A toad folds into a stone.
These flowers are all fangs. Comfort me, fury.
Wake me, witch, we'll do the dance of rotten sticks.

Shale loosens. Marl reaches into the field. Small birds pass over water.
Spirit, come near. This is only the edge of whiteness.
I can't laugh at a procession of dogs.

In the hour of ripeness the tree is barren.
The she-bear mopes under the hill.
Mother, mother, stir from your cave of sorrow.

A low mouth laps water. Weeds, weeds, how I love you.
The arbor is cooler. Farewell, farewell, fond worm.
The warm comes without sound.

2

Where's the eye?
The eye's in the sty.
The ear's not here
Beneath the hair.
When I took off my clothes
To find a nose,
There was only one shoe
For the waltz of To,
The pinch of Where.

61

Time for the flat-headed man. I recognize that listener,
Him with the platitudes and rubber doughnuts,
Melting at the knees, a varicose horror.
Hello, hello. My nerves knew you, dear boy.
Have you come to unhinge my shadow?
Last night I slept in the pits of a tongue.
The silver fish ran in and out of my special bindings;
I grew tired of the ritual of names and the assistant keeper of the
       mollusks:
Up over a viaduct I came, to the snakes and sticks of another winter,
A two-legged dog hunting a new horizon of howls.
The wind sharpened itself on a rock;
A voice sang:

    Pleasure on ground
    Has no sound,
    Easily maddens
    The uneasy man.

    Who, careless, slips
    In coiling ooze
    Is trapped to the lips,
    Leaves more than shoes;

    Must pull off clothes
    To jerk like a frog
    On belly and nose
    From the sucking bog.

My meat eats me. Who waits at the gate?
Mother of quartz, your words writhe into my ear.
Renew the light, lewd whisper.

3

The wasp waits.
        The edge cannot eat the center.
The grape glistens.
        The path tells little to the serpent.
An eye comes out of the wave.
        The journey from flesh is longest.
A rose sways least.
        The redeemer comes a dark way.

4

Morning-fair, follow me further back
Into that minnowy world of weeds and ditches,
When the herons floated high over the white houses,
And the little crabs slipped into silvery craters.
When the sun for me glinted the sides of a sand grain,
And my intent stretched over the buds at their first trembling.

That air and shine: and the flicker's loud summer call:
The bearded boards in the stream and the all of apples;
The glad hen on the hill; and the trellis humming.
Death was not. I lived in a simple drowse:
Hands and hair moved through a dream of wakening blossoms.
Rain sweetened the cave and the dove still called;
The flowers leaned on themselves, the flowers in hollows;
And love, love sang toward.

5

To have the whole air!—
The light, the full sun
Coming down on the flowerheads,
The tendrils turning slowly,
A slow snail-lifting, liquescent;
To be by the rose
Rising slowly out of its bed,
Still as a child in its first loneliness;
To see cyclamen veins become clearer in early sunlight,
And mist lifting out of the brown cat-tails;
To stare into the after-light, the glitter left on the lake's surface,
When the sun has fallen behind a wooded island;
To follow the drops sliding from a lifted oar,
Held up, while the rower breathes, and the small boat drifts quietly
          shoreward;
To know that light falls and fills, often without our knowing,
As an opaque vase fills to the brim from a quick pouring,
Fills and trembles at the edge yet does not flow over,
Still holding and feeding the stem of the contained flower.

[This sequence is continued in *Praise to the End!*, Part II, and concluded
with "O, Thou Opening, O" in *The Waking*.]

from PRAISE TO THE END!

1951

WHERE KNOCK IS OPEN WIDE

1

A kitten can
Bite with his feet;
Papa and Mamma
Have more teeth.

Sit and play
Under the rocker
Until the cows
All have puppies.

His ears haven't time.
Sing me a sleep-song, please.
A real hurt is soft.

Once upon a tree
I came across a time,
It wasn't even as
A ghoulie in a dream.

There was a mooly man
Who had a rubber hat
The funnier than that,—
He kept it in a can.

What's the time, papa-seed?
Everything has been twice.
My father is a fish.

2

I sing a small sing,
My uncle's away,
He's gone for always,
I don't care either.

I know who's got him,
They'll jump on his belly,
He won't be an angel,
I don't care either.

I know her noise.
Her neck has kittens.
I'll make a hole for her.
In the fire.

Winkie will yellow I sang.
Her eyes went kissing away
It was and it wasn't her there
I sang I sang all day.

3

I know it's an owl. He's making it darker.
Eat where you're at. I'm not a mouse.
Some stones are still warm.
I like soft paws.
Maybe I'm lost,
Or asleep.

A worm has a mouth.
Who keeps me last?
Fish me out.
Please.

God, give me a near. I hear flowers.
A ghost can't whistle.
I know! I know!
Hello happy hands.

4

We went by the river.
Water birds went ching. Went ching.
Stepped in wet. Over stones.
One, his nose had a frog,
But he slipped out.

I was sad for a fish.
Don't hit him on the boat, I said.
Look at him puff. He's trying to talk.
Papa threw him back.

Bullheads have whiskers.
And they bite.

  He watered the roses.
  His thumb had a rainbow.
  The stems said, Thank you.
  Dark came early.

That was before. I fell! I fell!
The worm has moved away.
My tears are tired.

Nowhere is out. I saw the cold.
Went to visit the wind. Where the birds die.
How high is have?
I'll be a bite. You be a wink.
Sing the snake to sleep.

5

  Kisses come back,
  I said to Papa;
  He was all whitey bones
  And skin like paper.

69

God's somewhere else,
I said to Mamma.
The evening came
A long long time.

I'm somebody else now.
Don't tell my hands.
Have I come to always? Not yet.
One father is enough.

Maybe God has a house.
But not here.

I NEED, I NEED

1

A deep dish. Lumps in it.
I can't taste my mother.
Hoo. I know the spoon.
Sit in my mouth.

A sneeze can't sleep.
Diddle we care
Couldly.

    Went down cellar,
    Talked to a faucet;
    The drippy water
    Had nothing to say.

    Whisper me over,
    Why don't you, begonia,
    There's no alas
    Where I live.

Scratched the wind with a stick.
The leaves liked it.
Do the dead bite?
Mamma, she's a sad fat.

70

A dove said dove all day.
A hat is a house.
I hid in his.

2

Even steven all is less:
I haven't time for sugar,
Put your finger in your face,
And there will be a booger.

A one is a two is
I know what you is:
You're not very nice,—
So touch my toes twice.

I know you are my nemesis
So bibble where the pebble is.
The Trouble is with No and Yes
As you can see I guess I guess.

I wish I was a pifflebob
I wish I was a funny
I wish I had ten thousand hats,
And made a lot of money.

Open a hole and see the sky:
A duck knows something
You and I don't.
Tomorrow is Friday.

Not you I need.
Go play with your nose.
Stay in the sun,
Snake-eyes.

3

Stop the larks. Can I have my heart back?
Today I saw a beard in a cloud.
The ground cried my name:
Good-bye for being wrong.
Love helps the sun.
But not enough.

4

When you plant, spit in the pot.
A pick likes to hit ice.
Hooray for me and the mice!—
The oats are all right.

Hear me, soft ears and roundy stones!
It's a dear life I can touch.
Who's ready for pink and frisk?
My hoe eats like a goat.

    Her feet said yes.
    It was all hay.
    I said to the gate,
    Who else knows
    What water does?
    Dew ate the fire.

I know another fire.
Has roots.

BRING THE DAY!

1

> Bees and lilies there were,
> Bees and lilies there were,
> Either to other,—
> Which would you rather?
> Bees and lilies were there.
>
> The green grasses,—would they?
> The green grasses?—
> She asked her skin
> To let me in:
> The far leaves were for it.

Forever is easy, she said.
How many angels do you know?—
And over by Algy's
Something came by me,
It wasn't a goose,
It wasn't a poodle.

> Everything's closer. Is this a cage?
> The chill's gone from the moon.
> Only the woods are alive.
> I can't marry the dirt.
>
> I'm a biscuit. I'm melted already.
> The white weather hates me.
> Why is how I like it.
> I can't catch a bush.

2

The herrings are awake.
What's all the singing between?—
Is it with whispers and kissing?—
I've listened into the least waves.
The grass says what the wind says:
Begin with the rock;
End with water.

When I stand, I'm almost a tree.
Leaves, do you like me any?
A swan needs a pond.
The worm and the rose
Both love
Rain.

3

O small bird wakening,
Light as a hand among blossoms,
Hardly any old angels are around any more.
The air's quiet under the small leaves.
The dust, the long dust, stays.
The spiders sail into summer.
It's time to begin!
To begin!

GIVE WAY, YE GATES

1

Believe me, knot of gristle, I bleed like a tree;
I dream of nothing but boards;
I could love a duck.

Such music in a skin!
A bird sings in the bush of your bones.
Tufty, the water's loose.
Bring me a finger. This dirt's lonesome for grass.
Are the rats dancing? The cats are.
And you, cat after great milk and vasty fishes,
A moon loosened from a stag's eye,
Twiced me nicely,—
In the green of my sleep,
In the green.

2

Mother of blue and the many changes of hay,
This tail hates a flat path.
I've let my nose out;
I could melt down a stone,—
How is it with the long birds?
May I look too, loved eye?
It's a wink beyond the world.
In the slow rain, who's afraid?
We're king and queen of the right ground.
I'll risk the winter for you.

You tree beginning to know,
You whisper of kidneys,
We'll swinge the instant!—
With jots and jogs and cinders on the floor:
The sea will be there, the great squashy shadows,
Biting themselves perhaps;
The shrillest frogs;
And the ghost of some great howl
Dead in a wall.

In the high-noon of thighs,
In the springtime of stones,
We'll stretch with the great stems.
We'll be at the business of what might be
Looking toward what we are.

3

You child with a beast's heart,
Make me a bird or a bear!
I've played with the fishes
Among the unwrinkling ferns
In the wake of a ship of wind;
But now the instant ages,
And my thought hunts another body.
I'm sad with the little owls.

4

Touch and arouse. Suck and sob. Curse and mourn.
It's a cold scrape in a low place.
The dead crow dries on a pole.
Shapes in the shade
Watch.

The mouth asks. The hand takes.
These wings are from the wrong nest.
Who stands in a hole
Never spills.

I hear the clap of an old wind.
The cold knows when to come.
What beats in me
I still bear.

The deep stream remembers:
Once I was a pond.
What slides away
Provides.

SENSIBILITY! O LA!

1

I'm the serpent of somebody else.
See! She's sleeping like a lake:
Glory to seize, I say.

In the fair night of some dim brain,
Thou wert marmorean-born.
I name thee: wench of things,
A true zephyr-haunted woodie.
The sea's unequal lengths announced thy birth
From a shell harder than horn.
Thy soft albino gaze
Spoke to my spirit.

It's queer enough here, perhaps.
Some rare new tedium's taking shape:
I smell the jumps ahead.
Can a cat milk a hen?

2

A whisper of what,
You round dog?—
Is the wasp tender?
John-of-the-thumb's jumping;
Commodities, here we come!

A shape comes to stay:
The long flesh.
I know the way out of a laugh;
I'm a twig to touch,
Pleased as a knife.

3

You all-of-a-sudden gods,
There's a ghost loose in the long grass!
My sweetheart's still in her cave.
I've waked the wrong wind:
I'm alone with my ribs;
The lake washes its stones.
You've seen me, prince of stinks,
Naked and entire.
Exalted? Yes,—
By the lifting of the tail of a neighbor's cat,
Or that old harpy secreting toads in her portmanteau.
Mamma! Put on your dark hood;
It's a long way to somewhere else.
The shade says: love the sun.
I have.
La, la,
The light turns.
The moon still abides.
I hear you, alien of the moon.
Is the sun under my arm?
My sleep deceives me.
Has the dark a door?
I'm somewhere else,—
I insist!
I am.

O LULL ME, LULL ME

1

One sigh stretches heaven.
In this, the diocese of mice,
Who's bishop of breathing?

How still she keeps herself.
Blessed be torpor.
Not all animals
Move about.

Tell me, great lords of sting,
Is it time to think?
When I say things fond,
I hear singing.
O my love's light as a duck
On a moon-forgotten wave!

The sea has many streets;
The beach rises with the waves.
I know my own bones:
This doxie doesn't do.

2

The air, the air provides.
Light fattens the rock.
Let's play before we forget!

A wish! A wish!
O lovely chink, O white
Way to another grace!—
I see my heart in the seed;
I breathe into a dream,
And the ground cries.
I'm crazed and graceless,
A winter-leaping frog.

Soothe me, great groans of underneath,
I'm still waiting for a foot.
The poke of the wind's close,
But I can't go leaping alone.
For you, my pond,
Rocking with small fish,
I'm an otter with only one nose:
I'm all ready to whistle;
I'm more than when I was born;
I could say hello to things;
I could talk to a snail;
I see what sings!
What sings!

II

PRAISE TO THE END!

1

It's dark in this wood, soft mocker.
For whom have I swelled like a seed?
What a bone-ache I have.
Father of tensions, I'm down to my skin at last.

It's a great day for the mice.
Prickle-me, tickle-me, close stems.
Bumpkin, he can dance alone.
Ooh, ooh, I'm a duke of eels.

Arch my back, pretty-bones, I'm dead at both ends.
Softly softly, you'll wake the clams.
I'll feed the ghost alone.
Father, forgive my hands.

The rings have gone from the pond.
The river's alone with its water.
All risings
Fall.

Where are you now, my bonny beating gristle,
My blue original dandy, numb with sugar?
Once I fished from the banks, leaf-light and happy:
On the rocks south of quiet, in the close regions of kissing,
I romped, lithe as a child, down the summery streets of my veins,
Strict as a seed, nippy and twiggy.
Now the water's low. The weeds exceed me.
It's necessary, among the flies and bananas, to keep a constant vigil,
For the attacks of false humility take sudden turns for the worse.
Lacking the candor of dogs, I kiss the departing air;
I'm untrue to my own excesses.

Rock me to sleep, the weather's wrong.
Speak to me, frosty beard.
Sing to me, sweet.

    Mips and ma the mooly moo,
    The likes of him is biting who,
    A cow's a care and who's a coo?—
    What footie does is final.

    My dearest dear my fairest fair,
    Your father tossed a cat in air,
    Though neither you nor I was there,—
    What footie does is final.

    Be large as an owl, be slick as a frog,
    Be good as a goose, be big as a dog,
    Be sleek as a heifer, be long as a hog,—
    What footie will do will be final.

I conclude! I conclude!
My dearest dust, I can't stay here.
I'm undone by the flip-flap of odious pillows.
An exact fall of waters has rendered me impotent.
I've been asleep in a bower of dead skin.
It's a piece of a prince I ate.
This salt can't warm a stone.
These lazy ashes.

3

The stones were sharp,
The wind came at my back;
Walked along the highway,
Mincing like a cat.

The sun came out;
The lake turned green;
Romped upon the goldy grass,
Aged thirteen.

The sky cracked open
The world I knew;
Lay like the cats do
Sniffing the dew.

I dreamt I was all bones;
The dead slept in my sleeve;
Sweet Jesus tossed me back:
I wore the sun with ease.

The several sounds were low;
The river ebbed and flowed:
Desire was winter-calm,
A moon away.

Such owly pleasures! Fish come first, sweet bird.
Skin's the least of me. Kiss this.
Is the eternal near, fondling?
I hear the sound of hands.

Can the bones breathe? This grave has an ear.
It's still enough for the knock of a worm.
I feel more than a fish.
Ghost, come closer.

Arch of air, my heart's original knock,
I'm awake all over:
I've crawled from the mire, alert as a saint or a dog;
I know the back-stream's joy, and the stone's eternal pulseless longing.
Felicity I cannot hoard.
My friend, the rat in the wall, brings me the clearest messages;
I bask in the bower of change;
The plants wave me in, and the summer apples;
My palm-sweat flashes gold;
Many astounds before, I lost my identity to a pebble;
The minnows love me, and the humped and spitting creatures.

I believe! I believe!—
In the sparrow, happy on gravel;
In the winter-wasp, pulsing its wings in the sunlight;
I have been somewhere else; I remember the sea-faced uncles.
I hear, clearly, the heart of another singing,
Lighter than bells,
Softer than water.

Wherefore, O birds and small fish, surround me.
Lave me, ultimate waters.
The dark showed me a face.
My ghosts are all gay.
The light becomes me.

UNFOLD! UNFOLD!

1

By snails, by leaps of frog, I came here, spirit.
Tell me, body without skin, does a fish sweat?
I can't crawl back through those veins,
I ache for another choice.
The cliffs! The cliffs! They fling me back.
Eternity howls in the last crags,
The field is no longer simple:
It's a soul's crossing time.
The dead speak noise.

2

It's time you stood up and asked
       —Or sat down and did.
A tongue without song
       —Can still whistle in a jug.
You're blistered all over
       —Who cares? The old owl?
When you find the wind
       —Look for the white fire.

3

What a whelm of proverbs, Mr. Pinch!
Are the entrails clear, immaculate cabbage?
The last time I nearly whispered myself away.
I was far back, farther than anybody else.
On the jackpine plains I hunted the bird nobody knows;
Fishing, I caught myself behind the ears.
Alone, in a sleep-daze, I stared at billboards;

I was privy to oily fungus and the algae of standing waters;
Honored, on my return, by the ancient fellowship of rotten stems.
I was pure as a worm on a leaf; I cherished the mold's children.
Beetles sweetened my breath.
I slept like an insect.

85

I met a collector of string, a shepherd of slow forms.
My mission became the salvation of minnows.
I stretched like a board, almost a tree.
Even thread had a speech.

Later, I did and I danced in the simple wood.
A mouse taught me how, I was a happy asker.
Quite-by-chance brought me many cookies.
I jumped in butter.
Hair had kisses.

4

Easy the life of the mouth. What a lust for ripeness!
All openings praise us, even oily holes.
The bulb unravels. Who's floating? Not me.
The eye perishes in the small vision.
What else has the vine loosened?
I hear a dead tongue halloo.

5

Sing, sing, you symbols! All simple creatures,
All small shapes, willow-shy,
In the obscure haze, sing!

A light song comes from the leaves.
A slow sigh says yes. And light sighs;
A low voice, summer-sad.
Is it you, cold father? Father,
For whom the minnows sang?

A house for wisdom; a field for revelation.
Speak to the stones, and the stars answer.
At first the visible obscures:
Go where light is.

This fat can't laugh.
Only my salt has a chance.
I'll seek my own meekness.
What grace I have is enough.
The lost have their own pace.
The stalks ask something else.
What the grave says,
The nest denies.

In their harsh thickets
The dead thrash.
They help.

I CRY, LOVE! LOVE!

1

Went weeping, little bones. But where?
Wasps come when I ask for pigeons.
The sister sands, they slipper soft away.
What else can befall?

    Delight me otherly, white spirit,—
    Some errand, obscure as the wind's circuit,
    A secret to jerk from the lips of a fish.
    Is circularity such a shame?
    A cat goes wider.

What's a thick? Two-by-two's a shape.
This toad could waltz on a drum;
I hear a most lovely huzza:
I'm king of the boops!

2

Reason? That dreary shed, that hutch for grubby schoolboys!
The hedgewren's song says something else.
I care for a cat's cry and the hugs, live as water.
I've traced these words in sand with a vestigial tail;
Now the gills are beginning to cry.
Such a sweet noise: I can't sleep for it.
Bless me and the maze I'm in!
Hello, thingy spirit.

    Mouse, mouse, come out of the ferns,
    And small mouths, stay your aimless cheeping:
    A lapful of apples sleeps in this grass.
    That anguish of concreteness!—
    The sun playing on loam,
    And the first dust of spring listing over backlots,—
    I proclaim once more a condition of joy.
    Walk into the wind, willie!

In a sodden place, all raps and knocks approve.
A dry cry comes from my own desert;
The bones are lonely.
Beginnings start without shade,
Thinner than minnows.
The live grass whirls with the sun,
Feet run over the simple stones,
There's time enough.
Behold, in the lout's eye,
Love.

3

I hear the owls, the soft callers, coming down from the hemlocks.
The bats weave in and out of the willows,
Wing-crooked and sure,
Downward and upward,
Dipping and veering close to the motionless water.

A fish jumps, shaking out flakes of moonlight.
A single wave starts lightly and easily shoreward,
Wrinkling between reeds in shallower water,
Lifting a few twigs and floating leaves,
Then washing up over small stones.

The shine on the face of the lake
Tilts, backward and forward.
The water recedes slowly,
Gently rocking.

Who untied the tree? I remember now.
We met in a nest. Before I lived.
The dark hair sighed.
We never enter
Alone.

1953

O, THOU OPENING, O

1

I'll make it; but it may take me.
The rat's my phase.
My left side's tender.
Read me the stream.

Dazzle me, dizzy aphorist.
Fling me a precept.
I'm a draft sleeping by a stick;
I'm lost in what I have.

 The Depth calls to the Height
  —Neither knows it.
 Those close to the Ground
  —Only stay out of the Wind.

Thrum-thrum, who can be equal to ease?
I've seen my father's face before
Deep in the belly of a thing to be.
The Devil isn't dead; he's just away.

Where's Ann? Where's Lou? Where's Jock-with-the-Wind?
Forgive me a minute, nymph.
I'll change the image, and my shoes.
A true mole wanders like a worm.

93

And now are we to have that pelludious Jesus-shimmer over all things, the animal's candid gaze, a shade less than feathers, light's broken speech revived, a ghostly going of tame bears, a bright moon on gleaming skin, a thing you cannot say to whisper and equal a Wound?

I'm tired of all that, Bag-Foot. I can hear small angels anytime. Who cares about the dance of dead underwear, or the sad waltz of paper bags? Who ever said God sang in your fat shape? You're not the only keeper of hay. That's a spratling's prattle. And don't be thinking you're simplicity's sweet thing, either. A leaf could drag you.

Where's the great rage of a rocking heart, the high rare true dangerous indignation? Let me persuade more slowly:

  The dark has its own light.
  A son has many fathers.
  Stand by a slow stream:
  Hear the sigh of what is.
  Be a pleased rock
  On a plain day.
  Waking's
  Kissing.
  Yes.

  You mean?—
  I can leap, true to the field,
  In the lily's sovereign right?
  Be a body lighted with love,
  Sad, in a singing-time?
  Or happy, correct as a hat?

  Oh, what a webby wonder I am!
  Swaying, would you believe,
  Like a sapling tree,
  Enough to please a cloud!

This frog's had another fall.
The old stalk still has a pulse;
I've crept from a cry.
The holy root wags the tail of a hill;
I'm true to soup, and happy to ask:
I sing the green, and things to come,
I'm king of another condition,
So alive I could die!
The ground's beating like flame!
You fat unnecessary hags,
You enemies of skin,—
A dolphin's at my door!
I'm twinkling like a twig!
The lark's my heart!
I'm wild with news!
My fancy's white!
I am my faces,
Love.

  Who reads in bed
    —Fornicates on the stove.
  An old dog
    —Should sleep on his paws.

See what the sweet harp says.
Should a song break a sleep?
The round home of a root,—
Is that the place to go?
I'm a tune dying
On harsh stone.
An Eye says,
Come.

I keep dreaming of bees.
This flesh has airy bones.
Going is knowing.
I see; I seek;
I'm near.
Be true,
Skin.

THE VISITANT

1

A cloud moved close. The bulk of the wind shifted.
A tree swayed over water.
A voice said:
Stay. Stay by the slip-ooze. Stay.

Dearest tree, I said, may I rest here?
A ripple made a soft reply.
I waited, alert as a dog.
The leech clinging to a stone waited;
And the crab, the quiet breather.

2

Slow, slow as a fish she came,
Slow as a fish coming forward,
Swaying in a long wave;
Her skirts not touching a leaf,
Her white arms reaching towards me.

She came without sound,
Without brushing the wet stones,
In the soft dark of early evening,
She came,
The wind in her hair,
The moon beginning.

I woke in the first of morning.
Staring at a tree, I felt the pulse of a stone.

Where's she now, I kept saying.
Where's she now, the mountain's downy girl?

But the bright day had no answer.
A wind stirred in a web of appleworms;
The tree, the close willow, swayed.

A LIGHT BREATHER

The spirit moves,
Yet stays:
Stirs as a blossom stirs,
Still wet from its bud-sheath,
Slowly unfolding,
Turning in the light with its tendrils;
Plays as a minnow plays,
Tethered to a limp weed, swinging,
Tail around, nosing in and out of the current,
Its shadows loose, a watery finger;
Moves, like the snail,
Still inward,
Taking and embracing its surroundings,
Never wishing itself away,
Unafraid of what it is,
A music in a hood,
A small thing,
Singing.

ELEGY FOR JANE
My Student, Thrown by a Horse

I remember the neckcurls, limp and damp as tendrils;
And her quick look, a sidelong pickerel smile;
And how, once startled into talk, the light syllables leaped for her,
And she balanced in the delight of her thought,
A wren, happy, tail into the wind,
Her song trembling the twigs and small branches.
The shade sang with her;
The leaves, their whispers turned to kissing;
And the mold sang in the bleached valleys under the rose.

Oh, when she was sad, she cast herself down into such a pure depth,
Even a father could not find her:
Scraping her cheek against straw;
Stirring the clearest water.

My sparrow, you are not here,
Waiting like a fern, making a spiny shadow.
The sides of wet stones cannot console me,
Nor the moss, wound with the last light.

If only I could nudge you from this sleep,
My maimed darling, my skittery pigeon.
Over this damp grave I speak the words of my love:
I, with no rights in this matter,
Neither father nor lover.

To seize, to seize,—
I know that dream.
Now my ardors sleep in a sleeve.
My eyes have forgotten.
Like the half-dead, I hug my last secrets.
O for some minstrel of what's to be,
A bird singing into the beyond,
The marrow of God, talking,
Full merry, a gleam
Gracious and bland,
On a bright stone.
Somewhere, among the ferns and birds,
The great swamps flash.
I would hold high converse
Where the winds gather,
And leap over my eye,
An old woman
Jumping in her shoes.
If only I could remember
The white grass bending away,
The doors swinging open,
The smells, the moment of hay,—
When I went to sea in a sigh,
In a boat of beautiful things.
The good day has gone:
The fair house, the high
Elm swinging around
With its deep shade, and birds.
I have listened close
For the thin sound in the windy chimney,
The fall of the last ash
From the dying ember.
I've become a sentry of small seeds,
Poking alone in my garden.
The stone walks, where are they?
Gone to bolster a road.
The shrunken soil
Has scampered away in a dry wind.
Once I was sweet with the light of myself,
A self-delighting creature,

Leaning over a rock,
My hair between me and the sun,
The waves rippling near me.
My feet remembered the earth,
The loam heaved me
That way and this.
My looks had a voice;
I was careless in growing.

If I were a young man,
I could roll in the dust of a fine rage.

The shadows are empty, the sliding externals.
The wind wanders around the house
On its way to the back pasture.
The cindery snow ticks over stubble.
My dust longs for the invisible.
I'm reminded to stay alive
By the dry rasp of the recurring inane,
The fine soot sifting through my south windows.
It is hard to care about corners,
And the sound of paper tearing.
I fall, more and more,
Into my own silences.
In the cold air,
The spirit
Hardens.

FOUR FOR SIR JOHN DAVIES

1. *The Dance*

Is that dance slowing in the mind of man
That made him think the universe could hum?
The great wheel turns its axle when it can;
I need a place to sing, and dancing-room,
And I have made a promise to my ears
I'll sing and whistle romping with the bears.

For they are all my friends: I saw one slide
Down a steep hillside on a cake of ice,—
Or was that in a book? I think with pride:
A caged bear rarely does the same thing twice
In the same way: O watch his body sway!—
This animal remembering to be gay.

I tried to fling my shadow at the moon,
The while my blood leaped with a wordless song.
Though dancing needs a master, I had none
To teach my toes to listen to my tongue.
But what I learned there, dancing all alone,
Was not the joyless motion of a stone.

I take this cadence from a man named Yeats;
I take it, and I give it back again:
For other tunes and other wanton beats
Have tossed my heart and fiddled through my brain.
Yes, I was dancing-mad, and how
That came to be the bears and Yeats would know.

2. *The Partner*

Between such animal and human heat
I find myself perplexed. What is desire?—
The impulse to make someone else complete?
That woman would set sodden straw on fire.
Was I the servant of a sovereign wish,
Or ladle rattling in an empty dish?

We played a measure with commingled feet:
The lively dead had taught us to be fond.
Who can embrace the body of his fate?
Light altered light along the living ground.
She kissed me close, and then did something else.
My marrow beat as wildly as my pulse.

I'd say it to my horse: we live beyond
Our outer skin. Who's whistling up my sleeve?
I see a heron prancing in his pond;
I know a dance the elephants believe.
The living all assemble! What's the cue?—
Do what the clumsy partner wants to do!

Things loll and loiter. Who condones the lost?
This joy outleaps the dog. Who cares? Who cares?
I gave her kisses back, and woke a ghost.
O what lewd music crept into our ears!
The body and the soul know how to play
In that dark world where gods have lost their way.

3. *The Wraith*

Incomprehensible gaiety and dread
Attended what we did. Behind, before,
Lay all the lonely pastures of the dead;
The spirit and the flesh cried out for more.
We two, together, on a darkening day
Took arms against our own obscurity.

Did each become the other in that play?
She laughed me out, and then she laughed me in;
In the deep middle of ourselves we lay;
When glory failed, we danced upon a pin.
The valley rocked beneath the granite hill;
Our souls looked forth, and the great day stood still.

There was a body, and it cast a spell,—
God pity those but wanton to the knees,—
The flesh can make the spirit visible;
We woke to find the moonlight on our toes.
In the rich weather of a dappled wood
We played with dark and light as children should.

102

What shape leaped forward at the sensual cry?—
Sea-beast or bird flung toward the ravaged shore?
Did space shake off an angel with a sigh?
We rose to meet the moon, and saw no more.
It was and was not she, a shape alone,
Impaled on light, and whirling slowly down.

4. *The Vigil*

Dante attained the purgatorial hill,
Trembled at hidden virtue without flaw,
Shook with a mighty power beyond his will,—
Did Beatrice deny what Dante saw?
All lovers live by longing, and endure:
Summon a vision and declare it pure.

Though everything's astonishment at last,
Who leaps to heaven at a single bound?
The links were soft between us; still, we kissed;
We undid chaos to a curious sound:
The waves broke easy, cried to me in white;
Her look was morning in the dying light.

The visible obscures. But who knows when?
Things have their thought: they are the shards of me;
I thought that once, and thought comes round again;
Rapt, we leaned forth with what we could not see.
We danced to shining; mocked before the black
And shapeless night that made no answer back.

The world is for the living. Who are they?
We dared the dark to reach the white and warm.
She was the wind when wind was in my way;
Alive at noon, I perished in her form.
Who rise from flesh to spirit know the fall:
The word outleaps the world, and light is all.

THE WAKING

I wake to sleep, and take my waking slow.
I feel my fate in what I cannot fear.
I learn by going where I have to go.

We think by feeling. What is there to know?
I hear my being dance from ear to ear.
I wake to sleep, and take my waking slow.

Of those so close beside me, which are you?
God bless the Ground! I shall walk softly there,
And learn by going where I have to go.

Light takes the Tree; but who can tell us how?
The lowly worm climbs up a winding stair;
I wake to sleep, and take my waking slow.

Great Nature has another thing to do
To you and me; so take the lively air,
And, lovely, learn by going where to go.

This shaking keeps me steady. I should know.
What falls away is always. And is near.
I wake to sleep, and take my waking slow.
I learn by going where I have to go.

1958

I

Lighter Pieces and Poems for Children

SONG FOR THE SQUEEZE-BOX

It wasn't Ernest; it wasn't Scott—
The boys I knew when I went to pot;
They didn't boast; they didn't snivel,
But stepped right up and swung at the Devil;
And after exchanging a punch or two,
They all sat down like me and you
—And began to drink up the money.

It wasn't the Colony; it wasn't the Stork;
It wasn't the joints in New York, New York;
But me and a girl friend learned a lot
In Ecorse, Toledo, and Wyandotte
—About getting rid of our money.

It was jump-in-the-hedge; it was wait-in-the-hall;
It was "Would you believe it—*fawther's* tall!"
(It turned out she hadn't a father at all)
—But how she could burn up the money!

A place I surely did like to go
Was the underbelly of Cicero;
And East St. Louis and Monongahela
Had the red-hot spots where you feel a
—Lot like losing some money.

Oh, the Synco Septet played for us then,
And even the boys turned out to be men
As we sat there drinking that bathtub gin
—And loosened up with our money.

It was Samoots Matuna and Bugs Moran;
It was Fade me another and Stick out your can;
It was Place and Show and Also Ran
—For you never won with that money.

Oh, it wasn't a crime, it wasn't a sin,
And nobody slipped me a Mickey Finn,
For whenever I could, I dealt them all in
—On that chunk of Grandpa's money.

It was Dead Man's Corner, it was Kelly's Stable;
It was Stand on your feet as long as you're able,
But many a man rolled under the table
—When he tried to drink up the money.

To some it may seem a sad thing to relate,
The dough I spent on Chippewa Kate,
For she finally left town on the Bay City freight
—When she thought I'd run out of money.

The doctors, the lawyers, the cops are all paid—
So I've got to get me a rich ugly old maid
Who isn't unwilling, who isn't afraid
—To help me eat up her money.

REPLY TO A LADY EDITOR

If the Poem (beginning "I knew a woman, lovely in her bones") in *The London Times Literary Supplement* has not appeared here, we offer you $75 for it. Could you wire us collect your answer?

> Sincerely yours,
> Alice S. Morris
> Literary Editor, *Harper's Bazaar*

Sweet Alice S. Morris, I *am* pleased, of course,
You take the *Times Supplement*, and read its verse,
And know that True Love is more than a Life-Force
—And so like my poem called *Poem*.

Dan Cupid, I tell you's a braw laddie-buck;
A visit from him is a piece of pure luck,
And should he arrive, why just lean yourself back
—And recite him my poem called *Poem*.

O print it, my dear, do publish it, yes,
That ladies their true natures never suppress,
When they come, dazedly, to the pretty pass
—Of acting my poem called *Poem*.

My darling, my dearest, most-honest-alive,
Just send me along that sweet seventy-five;
I'll continue to think on the nature of love,
—As I dance to my poem called *Poem*.

DINKY

O what's the weather in a Beard?
It's windy there, and rather weird,
And when you think the sky has cleared
  —Why, there is Dirty Dinky.

Suppose you walk out in a Storm,
With nothing on to keep you warm,
And then step barefoot on a Worm
  —Of course, it's Dirty Dinky.

As I was crossing a hot hot Plain,
I saw a sight that caused me pain,
You asked me before, I'll tell you again:
  —It *looked* like Dirty Dinky.

Last night you lay a-sleeping? No!
The room was thirty-five below;
The sheets and blankets turned to snow.
  —He'd got in: Dirty Dinky.

You'd better watch the things you do.
You'd better watch the things you do.
You're part of him; he's part of you
  —*You* may be Dirty Dinky.

THE COW

There Once was a Cow with a Double Udder.
When I think of it now, I just have to Shudder!
She was too much for One, you can bet your Life:
She had to be Milked by a Man and his Wife.

THE SERPENT

There was a Serpent who had to sing.
There was. There was.
He simply gave up Serpenting.
Because. Because.

He didn't like his Kind of Life;
He couldn't find a proper Wife;
He was a Serpent with a soul;
He got no Pleasure down his Hole.
And so, of course, he had to Sing,
And Sing he did, like Anything!
The Birds, they were, they were Astounded;
And various Measures Propounded
To stop the Serpent's Awful Racket:
They bought a Drum. He wouldn't Whack it.
They sent,—you always send,—to Cuba
And got a Most Commodious Tuba;
They got a Horn, they got a Flute,
But Nothing would suit.
He said, "Look, Birds, all this is futile:
I do *not* like to Bang or Tootle."
And then he cut loose with a Horrible Note
That practically split the Top of his Throat.
"You see," he said, with a Serpent's Leer,
"I'm Serious about my Singing Career!"
And the Woods Resounded with many a Shriek
As the Birds flew off to the End of Next Week.

THE SLOTH

In moving-slow he has no Peer.
You ask him something in his Ear,
He thinks about it for a Year;

And, then, before he says a Word
There, upside down (unlike a Bird),
He will assume that you have Heard—

A most Ex-as-per-at-ing Lug.
But should you call his manner Smug,
He'll sigh and give his Branch a Hug;

Then off again to Sleep he goes,
Still swaying gently by his Toes,
And you just *know* he knows he knows.

THE LADY AND THE BEAR

A Lady came to a Bear by a Stream.
"O why are you fishing that way?
Tell me, dear Bear there by the Stream,
Why are you fishing that way?"

"I am what is known as a Biddly Bear,—
That's why I'm fishing this way.
We Biddly's are Pee-culiar Bears.
And so,—I'm fishing this way.

"And besides, it seems there's a Law:
A most, most exactious Law
Says a Bear
Doesn't dare
Doesn't dare
Doesn't DARE
Use a Hook or a Line,
Or an old piece of Twine,
Not even the end of his Claw, Claw, Claw,
Not even the end of his Claw.
Yes, a Bear has to fish with his Paw, Paw, Paw.
A Bear has to fish with his Paw."

"O it's Wonderful how with a flick of your Wrist,
You can fish out a fish, out a fish, out a fish,
If I were a fish I just couldn't resist
You, when you are fishing that way, that way,
When you are fishing that way."

And at that the Lady slipped from the Bank
And fell in the Stream still clutching a Plank,
But the Bear just sat there until she Sank;
As he went on fishing his way, his way,
As he went on fishing his way.

Just the Bear...

As...

She loved the wind because the wind loved me.

II

II

Love Poems

THE DREAM

1

I met her as a blossom on a stem
Before she ever breathed, and in that dream
The mind remembers from a deeper sleep:
Eye learned from eye, cold lip from sensual lip.
My dream divided on a point of fire;
Light hardened on the water where we were;
A bird sang low; the moonlight sifted in;
The water rippled, and she rippled on.

2

She came toward me in the flowing air,
A shape of change, encircled by its fire.
I watched her there, between me and the moon;
The bushes and the stones danced on and on;
I touched her shadow when the light delayed;
I turned my face away, and yet she stayed.
A bird sang from the center of a tree;
She loved the wind because the wind loved me.

3

Love is not love until love's vulnerable.
She slowed to sigh, in that long interval.
A small bird flew in circles where we stood;
The deer came down, out of the dappled wood.
All who remember, doubt. Who calls that strange?
I tossed a stone, and listened to its plunge.
She knew the grammar of least motion, she
Lent me one virtue, and I live thereby.

4

She held her body steady in the wind;
Our shadows met, and slowly swung around;
She turned the field into a glittering sea;
I played in flame and water like a boy
And I swayed out beyond the white seafoam;
Like a wet log, I sang within a flame.
In that last while, eternity's confine,
I came to love, I came into my own.

ALL THE EARTH, ALL THE AIR

1

I stand with standing stones.
The stones stay where they are.
The twiny winders wind;
The little fishes move.
A ripple wakes the pond.

2

This joy's my fall. I am!—
A man rich as a cat,
A cat in the fork of a tree,
When she shakes out her hair.
I think of that, and laugh.

3

All innocence and wit,
She keeps my wishes warm;
When, easy as a beast,
She steps along the street,
I start to leave myself.

4

The truly beautiful,
Their bodies cannot lie:
The blossom stings the bee.
The ground needs the abyss,
Say the stones, say the fish.

A field recedes in sleep.
Where are the dead? Before me
Floats a single star.
A tree glides with the moon.
The field is mine! Is mine!

In a lurking-place I lurk,
One with the sullen dark.
What's hell but a cold heart?
But who, faced with her face,
Would not rejoice?

1

Love, love, a lily's my care,
She's sweeter than a tree.
Loving, I use the air
Most lovingly: I breathe;
Mad in the wind I wear
Myself as I should be,
All's even with the odd,
My brother the vine is glad.

Are flower and seed the same?
What do the great dead say?
Sweet Phoebe, she's my theme:
She sways whenever I sway.
"O love me while I am,
You green thing in my way!"
I cried, and the birds came down
And made my song their own.

Motion can keep me still:
She kissed me out of thought
As a lovely substance will;
She wandered; I did not:
I stayed, and light fell
Across her pulsing throat;
I stared, and a garden stone
Slowly became the moon.

The shallow stream runs slack;
The wind creaks slowly by;
Out of a nestling's beak
Comes a tremulous cry
I cannot answer back;
A shape from deep in the eye—
That woman I saw in a stone—
Keeps pace when I walk alone.

The sun declares the earth;
The stones leap in the stream;
On a wide plain, beyond
The far stretch of a dream,
A field breaks like the sea;
The wind's white with her name,
And I walk with the wind.

The dove's my will today.
She sways, half in the sun:
Rose, easy on a stem,
One with the sighing vine,
One to be merry with,
And pleased to meet the moon.
She likes wherever I am.

Passion's enough to give
Shape to a random joy:
I cry delight: I know
The root, the core of a cry.
Swan-heart, arbutus-calm,
She moves when time is shy:
Love has a thing to do.

A fair thing grows more fair;
The green, the springing green
Makes an intenser day
Under the rising moon;
I smile, no mineral man;
I bear, but not alone,
The burden of this joy.

3

Under a southern wind,
The birds and fishes move
North, in a single stream;
The sharp stars swing around;
I get a step beyond
The wind, and there I am,
I'm odd and full of love.

Wisdom, where is it found?—
Those who embrace, believe.
Whatever was, still is,
Says a song tied to a tree.
Below, on the ferny ground,
In rivery air, at ease,
I walk with my true love.

What time's my heart? I care.
I cherish what I have
Had of the temporal:
I am no longer young
But the winds and waters are;
What falls away will fall;
All things bring me to love.

4

The breath of a long root,
The shy perimeter
Of the unfolding rose,
The green, the altered leaf,
The oyster's weeping foot,
And the incipient star—
Are part of what she is.
She wakes the ends of life.

Being myself, I sing
The soul's immediate joy.
Light, light, where's my repose?
A wind wreathes round a tree.
A thing is done: a thing
Body and spirit know
When I do what she does:
Creaturely creature, shel—

I kiss her moving mouth,
Her swart hilarious skin;
She breaks my breath in half;
She frolics like a beast;
And I dance round and round,
A fond and foolish man,
And see and suffer myself
In another being, at last.

I KNEW A WOMAN

I knew a woman, lovely in her bones,
When small birds sighed, she would sigh back at them;
Ah, when she moved, she moved more ways than one:
The shapes a bright container can contain!
Of her choice virtues only gods should speak,
Or English poets who grew up on Greek
(I'd have them sing in chorus, cheek to cheek).

How well her wishes went! She stroked my chin,
She taught me Turn, and Counter-turn, and Stand;
She taught me Touch, that undulant white skin;
I nibbled meekly from her proffered hand;
She was the sickle; I, poor I, the rake,
Coming behind her for her pretty sake
(But what prodigious mowing we did make).

Love likes a gander, and adores a goose:
Her full lips pursed, the errant note to seize;
She played it quick, she played it light and loose;
My eyes, they dazzled at her flowing knees;
Her several parts could keep a pure repose,
Or one hip quiver with a mobile nose
(She moved in circles, and those circles moved).

Let seed be grass, and grass turn into hay:
I'm martyr to a motion not my own;
What's freedom for? To know eternity.
I swear she cast a shadow white as stone.
But who would count eternity in days?
These old bones live to learn her wanton ways:
(I measure time by how a body sways).

THE VOICE

One feather is a bird,
I claim; one tree, a wood;
In her low voice I heard
More than a mortal should;
And so I stood apart,
Hidden in my own heart.

And yet I roamed out where
Those notes went, like the bird,
Whose thin song hung in air,
Diminished, yet still heard:
I lived with open sound,
Aloft, and on the ground.

That ghost was my own choice,
The shy cerulean bird;
It sang with her true voice,
And it was I who heard
A slight voice reply;
I heard; and only I.

Desire exults the ear:
Bird, girl, and ghostly tree,
The earth, the solid air—
Their slow song sang in me;
The long noon pulsed away,
 Like any summer day.

SHE

I think the dead are tender. Shall we kiss?—
My lady laughs, delighting in what is.
If she but sighs, a bird puts out its tongue.
She makes space lonely with a lovely song.
She lilts a low soft language, and I hear
Down long sea-chambers of the inner ear.

We sing together; we sing mouth to mouth.
The garden is a river flowing south.
She cries out loud the soul's own secret joy;
She dances, and the ground bears her away.
She knows the speech of light, and makes it plain
A lively thing can come to life again.

I feel her presence in the common day,
In that slow dark that widens every eye.
She moves as water moves, and comes to me,
Stayed by what was, and pulled by what would be.

THE OTHER

What is she, while I live?—
Who plagues me with her Shape,
Lifting a nether Lip
Lightly: so buds unleave;
But if I move too close,
Who busks me on the Nose?

Is she what I become?
Is this my final Face?
I find her every place;
She happens, time on time—
My Nose feels for my Toe;
Nature's too much to know.

Who can surprise a thing
Or come to love alone?
A lazy natural man,
I loll, I loll, all Tongue.
She moves, and I adore:
Motion can do no more.

A child stares past a fire
With the same absent gaze:
I know her careless ways!—
Desire hides from desire.
Aging, I sometimes weep,
Yet still laugh in my sleep.

THE SENTENTIOUS MAN

1

Spirit and nature beat in one breast-bone—
I saw a virgin writhing in the dirt—
The serpent's heart sustains the loveless stone:
My indirection found direction out.

Pride in fine lineaments precedes a fall;
True lechers love the flesh, and that is all.

2

We did not fly the flesh. Who does, when young?
A fire leaps on itself: I know that flame.
Some rages save us. Did I rage too long?
The spirit knows the flesh it must consume.

The dream's an instant that calls up her face.
She changed me ice to fire, and fire to ice.

3

Small waves repeat the mind's slow sensual play.
I stay alive, both in and out of time,
By listening to the spirit's smallest cry;
In the long night, I rest within her name—

As if a lion knelt to kiss a rose,
Astonished into passionate repose.

Though all's in motion, who is passing by?
The after-image never stays the same.
There was a thicket where I went to die,
And there I thrashed, my thighs and face aflame.

But my least motion changed into a song,
And all dimensions quivered to one thing.

An exultation takes us outside life:
I can delight in my own hardihood;
I taste my sister when I kiss my wife;
I drink good liquor when my luck is good.

A drunkard drinks, and belches in his drink;
Such ardor tames eternity, I think.

Is pain a promise? I was schooled in pain,
And found out all I could of all desire;
I weep for what I'm like when I'm alone
In the deep center of the voice and fire.

I know the motion of the deepest stone.
Each one's himself, yet each one's everyone.

I'm tired of brooding on my neighbor's soul;
My friends become more Christian, year by year.
Small waters run toward a miry hole—
That's not a thing I'm saying with a sneer—

For water moves until it's purified,
And the weak bridegroom strengthens in his bride.

THE PURE FURY

1

Stupor of knowledge lacking inwardness—
What book, O learned man, will set me right?
Once I read nothing through a fearful night,
For every meaning had grown meaningless.
Morning, I saw the world with second sight,
As if all things had died, and rose again.
I touched the stones, and they had my own skin.

2

The pure admire the pure, and live alone;
I love a woman with an empty face.
Parmenides put Nothingness in place;
She tries to think, and it flies loose again.
How slow the changes of a golden mean:
Great Boehme rooted all in Yes and No;
At times my darling squeaks in pure Plato.

3

How terrible the need for solitude:
That appetite for life so ravenous
A man's a beast prowling in his own house,
A beast with fangs, and out for his own blood
Until he finds the thing he almost was
When the pure fury first raged in his head
And trees came closer with a denser shade.

Dream of a woman, and a dream of death:
The light air takes my being's breath away;
I look on white, and it turns into gray—
When will that creature give me back my breath?
I live near the abyss. I hope to stay
Until my eyes look at a brighter sun
As the thick shade of the long night comes on.

THE RENEWAL

1

What glories would we? Motions of the soul?
The centaur and the sibyl romp and sing
Within the reach of my imagining:
Such affirmations are perpetual.
I teach my sighs to lengthen into songs,
Yet, like a tree, endure the shift of things.

2

The night wind rises. Does my father live?
Dark hangs upon the waters of the soul;
My flesh is breathing slower than a wall.
Love alters all. Unblood my instinct, love.
These waters drowse me into sleep so kind
I walk as if my face would kiss the wind.

3

Sudden renewal of the self—from where?
A raw ghost drinks the fluid in my spine;
I know I love, yet know not where I am;
I paw the dark, the shifting midnight air.
Will the self, lost, be found again? In form?
I walk the night to keep my five wits warm.

4

Dry bones! Dry bones! I find my loving heart,
Illumination brought to such a pitch
I see the rubblestones begin to stretch
As if reality had split apart
And the whole motion of the soul lay bare:
I find that love, and I am everywhere.

THE SENSUALISTS

"There is no place to turn," she said,
  "You have me pinned so close;
My hair's all tangled on your head,
  My back is just one bruise;
I feel we're breathing with the dead;
  O angel, let me loose!"

And she was right, for there beside
  The gin and cigarettes,
A woman stood, pure as a bride,
  Affrighted from her wits,
And breathing hard, as that man rode
  Between those lovely tits.

"My shoulder's bitten from your teeth;
  What's that peculiar smell?
No matter which one is beneath,
  Each is an animal,"—
The ghostly figure sucked its breath,
  And shuddered toward the wall;
Wrapped in the tattered robe of death,
  It tiptoed down the hall.

"The bed itself begins to quake,
  I hate this sensual pen;
My neck, if not my heart, will break
  If we do this again,"—
Then each fell back, limp as a sack,
  Into the world of men.

LOVE'S PROGRESS

1

The possibles we dare!
O rare propinquity!—
I have considered and found
A mouth I cannot leave.
The great gods arch my bones.

2

The long veins of the vine
Journey around a tree;
Light strides the rose;
A woman's naked in water,
And I know where she is.

3

True, she can think a bird
Until it broods in her eyes.
Love me, my violence,
Light of my spirit, light
Beyond the look of love.

4

It's midnight on the mouse,
The rabbit, and the wren;
A log sings in its flame.
Father, I'm far from home,
And I have gone nowhere.

5

The close dark hugs me hard,
And all the birds are stone.
I fear for my own joy;
I fear myself in the field,
For I would drown in fire.

THE SURLY ONE

1

When true love broke my heart in half,
I took the whiskey from the shelf,
And told my neighbors when to laugh.
I keep a dog, and bark myself.

2

Ghost cries out to ghost—
But who's afraid of that?
I fear those shadows most
That start from my own feet.

PLAINT

Day after somber day,
I think my neighbors strange;
In hell there is no change.
Where's my eternity
Of inward blessedness?
I lack plain tenderness.

Where is the knowledge that
Could bring me to my God?
Not on this dusty road
Or afternoon of light
Diminished by the haze
Of late November days.

I lived with deep roots once:
Have I forgotten their ways—
The gradual embrace
Of lichen around stones?
Death is a deeper sleep,
And I delight in sleep.

THE SWAN

1

I study out a dark similitude: *[handwritten: semblance; counter-person]*
Her image fades, yet does not disappear—
Must I stay tangled in that lively hair?
Is there no way out of that coursing blood?
A dry soul's wisest. O, I am not dry!
My darling does what I could never do:
She sighs me white, a Socrates of snow.

We think too long in terms of what to be;
I live, alive and certain as a bull;
A casual man, I keep my casual word,
Yet whistle back at every whistling bird.
A man alive, from all light I must fall.
I am my father's son, I am John Donne
Whenever I see her with nothing on.

2

[handwritten: moon v. tides; Poet v. similitude (genwoman)]
[handwritten: moon v. tides (gravity)]

The moon draws back its waters from the shore.
By the lake's edge, I see a silver swan,
And she is what I would. In this light air,
Lost opposites bend down—
Sing of that nothing of which all is made,
Or listen into silence, like a god.

135

MEMORY

1

In the slow world of dream,
We breathe in unison.
The outside dies within,
And she knows all I am.

2

She turns, as if to go,
Half-bird, half-animal.
The wind dies on the hill.
Love's all. Love's all I know.

3

A doe drinks by a stream,
A doe and its fawn.
When I follow after them,
The grass changes to stone.

III

Voices and Creatures

"THE SHIMMER OF EVIL"
Louise Bogan

The weather wept, and all the trees bent down;
Bent down their birds: the light waves took the waves;
Each single substance gliddered to the stare;
Each vision purely, purely was its own:
—There was no light; there was no light at all:

Far from the mirrors all the bushes rang
With their hard snow; leaned on the lonely eye;
Cold evil twinkled tighter than a string; a fire
Hung down: And I was only I.
—There was no light; there was no light at all:

Each cushion found itself a field of pins,
Prickling pure wishes with confusion's ire;
Hope's holy wrists: the little burning boys
Cried out their lives an instant and were free.
—There was no light; there was no light at all.

ELEGY

1

Should every creature be as I have been,
There would be reason for essential sin;
I have myself an inner weight of woe
That God himself can scarcely bear.

2

Each wills his death: I am convinced of that;
You were too lonely for another fate.
I have myself an inner weight of woe
That Christ, securely bound, could bear.

3

Thus I; and should these reasons fly apart,
I know myself, my seasons, and I KNOW.
I have myself one crumbling skin to show;
God could believe: I am here to fear.

4

What you survived I shall believe: the Heat,
Scars, Tempests, Floods, the Motion of Man's Fate;
I have myself, and bear its weight of woe
That God that God leans down His heart to hear.

THE BEAST

I came to a great door,
Its lintel overhung
With burr, bramble, and thorn;
And when it swung, I saw
A meadow, lush and green.

And there a great beast played,
A sportive, aimless one,
A shred of bone its horn,
And colloped round with fern.
It looked at me; it stared.

Swaying, I took its gaze;
Faltered; rose up again;
Rose but to lurch and fall,
Hard, on the gritty sill,
I lay; I languished there.

When I raised myself once more,
The great round eyes had gone.
The long lush grass lay still;
And I wept there, alone.

THE SONG

1

I met a ragged man;
He looked beyond me when
I tried to meet his eyes.
What have I done to you?
I cried, and backed away.
Dust in a corner stirred,
And the walls stretched wide.

2

I went running down a road,
In a country of bleak stone,
And shocks of ragged corn;
When I stayed for breath, I lay
With the saxifrage and fern
At the edge of a raw field.
I stared at a fissure of ground
Ringed round with crumbled clay:
The old house of a crab;
Stared, and began to sing.

3

I sang to whatever had been
Down in that watery hole:
I wooed with a low tune;
You could say I was mad.
And a wind woke in my hair,
And the sweat poured from my face,
When I heard, or thought I heard,
Another join my song
With the small voice of a child,
Close, and yet far away.

Mouth upon mouth, we sang,
My lips pressed upon stone.

THE EXORCISM

1

The grey sheep came. I ran,
My body half in flame.
(Father of flowers, who
Dares face the thing he is?)

As if pure being woke,
The dust rose and spoke;
A shape cried from a cloud,
Cried to my flesh out loud.

(And yet I was not there,
But down long corridors,
My own, my secret lips
Babbling in urinals.)

2

In a dark wood I saw—
I saw my several selves
Come running from the leaves,
Lewd, tiny, careless lives
That scuttled under stones,
Or broke, but would not go.
I turned upon my spine,
I turned and turned again,
A cold God-furious man
Writhing until the last
Forms of his secret life
Lay with the dross of death.

I was myself, alone.

I broke from that low place
Breathing a slower breath,
Cold, in my own dead salt.

THE SMALL

The small birds swirl around;
The high cicadas chirr;
A towhee pecks the ground;
I look at the first star:
My heart held to its joy,
This whole September day.

The moon goes to the full;
The moon goes slowly down;
The wood becomes a wall.
Far things draw closer in.
A wind moves through the grass,
Then all is as it was.

What rustles in the fern?
I feel my flesh divide.
Things lost in sleep return
As if out of my side,
On feet that make no sound
Over the sodden ground.

The small shapes drowse: I live
To woo the fearful small;
What moves in grass I love—
The dead will not lie still,
And things throw light on things,
And all the stones have wings.

A WALK IN LATE SUMMER

1

A gull rides on the ripples of a dream,
White upon white, slow-settling on a stone;
Across my lawn the soft-backed creatures come;
In the weak light they wander, each alone.
Bring me the meek, for I would know their ways;
I am a connoisseur of midnight eyes.
The small! The small! I hear them singing clear
On the long banks, in the soft summer air.

2

What is there for the soul to understand?
The slack face of the dismal pure inane?
The wind dies down; my will dies with the wind,
God's in that stone, or I am not a man!
Body and soul transcend appearances
Before the caving-in of all that is;
I'm dying piecemeal, fervent in decay;
My moments linger—that's eternity.

3

A late rose ravages the casual eye,
A blaze of being on a central stem.
It lies upon us to undo the lie
Of living merely in the realm of time.
Existence moves toward a certain end—
A thing all earthly lovers understand.
That dove's elaborate way of coming near
Reminds me I am dying with the year.

A tree arises on a central plain—
It is no trick of change or chance of light.
A tree all out of shape from wind and rain,
A tree thinned by the wind obscures my sight.
The long day dies; I walked the woods alone;
Beyond the ridge two wood thrush sing as one.
Being delights in being, and in time.
The evening wraps me, steady as a flame.

SNAKE

I saw a young snake glide
Out of the mottled shade
And hang, limp on a stone:
A thin mouth, and a tongue
Stayed, in the still air.

It turned; it drew away;
Its shadow bent in half;
It quickened, and was gone.

I felt my slow blood warm.
I longed to be that thing,
The pure, sensuous form.

And I may be, some time.

SLUG

How I loved one like you when I was little!—
With his stripes of silver and his small house on his back,
Making a slow journey around the well-curb.
I longed to be like him, and was,
In my way, close cousin
To the dirt, my knees scrubbing
The gravel, my nose wetter than his.

When I slip, just slightly, in the dark,
I know it isn't a wet leaf,
But you, loose toe from the old life,
The cold slime come into being,
A fat, five-inch appendage
Creeping slowly over the wet grass,
Eating the heart out of my garden.

And you refuse to die decently!—
Flying upward through the knives of my lawnmower
Like pieces of smoked eel or raw oyster,
And I go faster in my rage to get done with it,
Until I'm scraping and scratching at you, on the doormat,
The small dead pieces sticking under an instep;
Or, poisoned, dragging a white skein of spittle over a path—
Beautiful, in its way, like quicksilver—
You shrink to something less,
A rain-drenched fly or spider.

I'm sure I've been a toad, one time or another.
With bats, weasels, worms—I rejoice in the kinship.
Even the caterpillar I can love, and the various vermin.
But as for you, most odious—
Would Blake call you holy?

THE SISKINS

The bank swallows veer and dip,
Diving down at my windows,
Then flying almost straight upward,
Like bats in daytime,
And their shadows, bigger,
Race over the thick grass;
And the finches pitch through the air, twittering;
And the small mad siskins flit by,
Flying upward in little skips and erratic leaps;
Or they sit sideways on limber dandelion stems,
Bending them down to the ground;
Or perch and peck at larger flower-crowns,
Springing, one to another,
The last-abandoned stalk always quivering
Back into straightness;
Or they fling themselves against tree trunks,
Scuttling down and around like young squirrels,
Birds furious as bees.

Now they move all together!—
These airy hippety-hop skippers,
Light as seed blowing off thistles!
And I seem to lean forward,
As my eyes follow after
Their sunlit leaping.

IV

The Dying Man

IN MEMORIAM: W. B. YEATS

THE DYING MAN

1. *His Words*

I heard a dying man
Say to his gathered kin,
"My soul's hung out to dry,
Like a fresh-salted skin;
I doubt I'll use it again.

"What's done is yet to come;
The flesh deserts the bone,
But a kiss widens the rose;
I know, as the dying know,
Eternity is Now.

"A man sees, as he dies,
Death's possibilities;
My heart sways with the world.
I am that final thing,
A man learning to sing."

2. *What Now?*

Caught in the dying light,
I thought myself reborn.
My hands turn into hooves.
I wear the leaden weight
Of what I did not do.

Places great with their dead,
The mire, the sodden wood,
Remind me to stay alive.
I am the clumsy man
The instant ages on.

I burned the flesh away,
In love, in lively May.
I turn my look upon
Another shape than hers
Now, as the casement blurs.

In the worst night of my will,
I dared to question all,
And would the same again.
What's beating at the gate?
Who's come can wait.

3. *The Wall*

A ghost comes out of the unconscious mind
To grope my sill: It moans to be reborn!
The figure at my back is not my friend;
The hand upon my shoulder turns to horn.
I found my father when I did my work,
Only to lose myself in this small dark.

Though it reject dry borders of the seen,
What sensual eye can keep an image pure,
Leaning across a sill to greet the dawn?
A slow growth is a hard thing to endure.
When figures out of obscure shadow rave,
All sensual love's but dancing on a grave.

148

The wall has entered: I must love the wall,
A madman staring at perpetual night,
A spirit raging at the visible.
I breathe alone until my dark is bright.
Dawn's where the white is. Who would know the dawn
When there's a dazzling dark behind the sun?

4. *The Exulting*

Once I delighted in a single tree;
The loose air sent me running like a child—
I love the world; I want more than the world,
Or after-image of the inner eye.
Flesh cries to flesh; and bone cries out to bone;
I die into this life, alone yet not alone.

Was it a god his suffering renewed?—
I saw my father shrinking in his skin;
He turned his face: there was another man,
Walking the edge, loquacious, unafraid.
He quivered like a bird in birdless air,
Yet dared to fix his vision anywhere.

Fish feed on fish, according to their need:
My enemies renew me, and my blood
Beats slower in my careless solitude.
I bare a wound, and dare myself to bleed.
I think a bird, and it begins to fly.
By dying daily, I have come to be.

All exultation is a dangerous thing.
I see you, love, I see you in a dream;
I hear a noise of bees, a trellis hum,
And that slow humming rises into song.
A breath is but a breath: I have the earth;
I shall undo all dying by my death.

5. *They Sing, They Sing*

All women loved dance in a dying light—
The moon's my mother: how I love the moon!
Out of her place she comes, a dolphin one,
Then settles back to shade and the long night.
A beast cries out as if its flesh were torn,
And that cry takes me back where I was born.

Who thought love but a motion in the mind?
Am I but nothing, leaning towards a thing?
I'll scare myself with sighing, or I'll sing;
Descend, O gentlest light, descend, descend.
O sweet field far ahead, I hear your birds,
They sing, they sing, but still in minor thirds.

I've the lark's word for it, who sings alone:
What's seen recedes; Forever's what we know!—
Eternity defined, and strewn with straw,
The fury of the slug beneath the stone.
The vision moves, and yet remains the same.
In heaven's praise, I dread the thing I am.

The edges of the summit still appall
When we brood on the dead or the beloved;
Nor can imagination do it all
In this last place of light: he dares to live
Who stops being a bird, yet beats his wings
Against the immense immeasurable emptiness of things.

V

Meditations of an Old Woman

FIRST MEDITATION

1

On love's worst ugly day,
The weeds hiss at the edge of the field,
The small winds make their chilly indictments.
Elsewhere, in houses, even pails can be sad;
While stones loosen on the obscure hillside,
And a tree tilts from its roots,
Toppling down an embankment.

The spirit moves, but not always upward,
While animals eat to the north,
And the shale slides an inch in the talus,
The bleak wind eats at the weak plateau,
And the sun brings joy to some.
But the rind, often, hates the life within.

How can I rest in the days of my slowness?
I've become a strange piece of flesh,
Nervous and cold, bird-furtive, whiskery,
With a cheek soft as a hound's ear.
What's left is light as a seed;
I need an old crone's knowing.

151

Often I think of myself as riding—
Alone, on a bus through western country.
I sit above the back wheels, where the jolts are hardest,
And we bounce and sway along toward the midnight,
The lights tilting up, skyward, as we come over a little rise,
Then down, as we roll like a boat from a wave-crest.

All journeys, I think, are the same:
The movement is forward, after a few wavers,
And for a while we are all alone,
Busy, obvious with ourselves,
The drunken soldier, the old lady with her peppermints;
And we ride, we ride, taking the curves
Somewhat closer, the trucks coming
Down from behind the last ranges,
Their black shapes breaking past;
And the air claps between us,
Blasting the frosted windows,
And I seem to go backward,
Backward in time:

Two song sparrows, one within a greenhouse,
Shuttling its throat while perched on a wind-vent,
And another, outside, in the bright day,
With a wind from the west and the trees all in motion.
One sang, then the other,
The songs tumbling over and under the glass,
And the men beneath them wheeling in dirt to the cement
benches,
The laden wheelbarrows creaking and swaying,
And the up-spring of the plank when a foot left the runway.

Journey within a journey:
The ticket mislaid or lost, the gate
Inaccessible, the boat always pulling out
From the rickety wooden dock,
The children waving;
Or two horses plunging in snow, their lines tangled,
A great wooden sleigh careening behind them,
Swerving up a steep embankment.
For a moment they stand above me,

Their black skins shuddering:
Then they lurch forward,
Lunging down a hillside.

3

As when silt drifts and sifts down through muddy pond-water,
Settling in small beads around weeds and sunken branches,
And one crab, tentative, hunches himself before moving along the
        bottom,
Grotesque, awkward, his extended eyes looking at nothing in par-
        ticular,
Only a few bubbles loosening from the ill-matched tentacles,
The tail and smaller legs slipping and sliding slowly backward—
So the spirit tries for another life,
Another way and place in which to continue;
Or a salmon, tired, moving up a shallow stream,
Nudges into a back-eddy, a sandy inlet,
Bumping against sticks and bottom-stones, then swinging
Around, back into the tiny maincurrent, the rush of brownish-white
        water,
Still swimming forward—
So, I suppose, the spirit journeys.

4

I have gone into the waste lonely places
Behind the eye; the lost acres at the edge of smoky cities.
What's beyond never crumbles like an embankment,
Explodes like a rose, or thrusts wings over the Caribbean.
There are no pursuing forms, faces on walls:
Only the motes of dust in the immaculate hallways,
The darkness of falling hair, the warnings from lint and spiders,
The vines graying to a fine powder.
There is no riven tree, or lamb dropped by an eagle.

There are still times, morning and evening:
The cerulean, high in the elm,
Thin and insistent as a cicada,
And the far phoebe, singing,
The long plaintive notes floating down,

Drifting through leaves, oak and maple,
Or the whippoorwill, along the smoky ridges,
A single bird calling and calling;
A fume reminds me, drifting across wet gravel;
A cold wind comes over stones;
A flame, intense, visible,
Plays over the dry pods,
Runs fitfully along the stubble,
Moves over the field,
Without burning.
     In such times, lacking a god,
     I am still happy.

I'M HERE

1

Is it enough?—
The sun loosening the frost on December windows,
The glitter of wet in the first of morning?
The sound of voices, young voices, mixed with sleighbells,
Coming across snow in early evening?

Outside, the same sparrows bicker in the eaves.
I'm tired of tiny noises:
The April cheeping, the vireo's insistence,
The prattle of the young no longer pleases.
Behind the child's archness
Lurks the bad animal.

    —How needles and corners perplex me!
      Dare I shrink to a hag,
      The worst surprise a corner could have,
      A witch who sleeps with her horse?
      Some fates are worse.

2

I was queen of the vale—
For a short while,
Living all my heart's summer alone,
Ward of my spirit,
Running through high grasses,
My thighs brushing against flower-crowns;
Leaning, out of all breath,
Bracing my back against a sapling,
Making it quiver with my body;

155

At the stream's edge, trailing a vague finger;
Flesh-awkward, half-alive,
Fearful of high places, in love with horses;
In love with stuffs, silks,
Rubbing my nose in the wool of blankets;
Bemused; pleased to be;
Mindful of cries,
The meaningful whisper,
The wren, the catbird.

> So much of adolescence is an ill-defined dying,
> An intolerable waiting,
> A longing for another place and time,
> Another condition.

I stayed: a willow to the wind.
The bats twittered at noon.
The swallows flew in and out of the smokeless chimneys.
I sang to the edges of flame,
My skin whiter in the soft weather,
My voice softer.

3

I remember walking down a path,
Down wooden steps toward a weedy garden;
And my dress caught on rose-brier.
When I bent to untangle myself,
The scent of the half-opened buds came up over me.
I thought I was going to smother.

> In the slow coming-out of sleep,
> On the sill of the eyes, something flutters,
> A thing we feel at evening, and by doors,
> Or when we stand at the edge of a thicket,
> And the ground-chill comes closer to us,
> From under the dry leaves,
> A beachy wetness.

The body, delighting in thresholds,
Rocks in and out of itself.
A bird, small as a leaf,
Sings in the first
Sunlight.

And the time I was so sick—
The whole place shook whenever I got a chill—
I closed my eyes, and saw small figures dancing,
A congress of tree-shrews and rats,
Romping around a fire,
Jumping up and down on their hind feet,
Their forepaws joined together, like hands—
They seemed very happy.

    In my grandmother's inner eye,
    So she told me when I was little,
    A bird always kept singing.
    She was a serious woman.

4

My geranium is dying, for all I can do,
Still leaning toward the last place the sun was.
I've tried I don't know how many times to replant it.
But these roses: I can wear them by looking away.
The eyes rejoice in the act of seeing and the fresh after-image;
Without staring like a lout, or a moping adolescent;
Without commotion.
Look at the far trees at the end of the garden.
The flat branch of that hemlock holds the last of the sun,
Rocking it, like a sun-struck pond,
In a light wind.

    I prefer the still joy:
    The wasp drinking at the edge of my cup;
    A snake lifting its head;
    A snail's music.

5

What's weather to me? Even carp die in this river.
I need a pond with small eels. And a windy orchard.
I'm no midge of that and this. The dirt glitters like salt.
Birds are around. I've all the singing I would.
I'm not far from a stream.
It's not my first dying.
I can hold this valley,
Loose in my lap,
In my arms.

    If the wind means me,
    I'm here!
    Here.

HER BECOMING

1

I have learned to sit quietly,
Watching the wind riffle the backs of small birds,
Chirping with fleas in the sand,
My shape a levity—Yes!—
A mad hen in a far corner of the dark,
Still taking delight in nakedness,
In the sun, busy at a young body,
In the rain, slackening on a summer field;
In the back of my mind, running with the rolling water,
My breast wild as the waves.

    I see a shape, lighted with love,
    Light as a petal falling upon stone.
    From the folds of my skin, I sing,
    The air still, the ground alive,
    The earth itself a tune.

How sweetly I abide. Am I a bird?
Soft, soft, the snow's not falling. What's a seed?
A face floats in the ferns. Do maimed gods walk?
A voice keeps rising in my early sleep,
A muffled voice, a low sweet watery noise.
Dare I embrace a ghost from my own breast?
A spirit plays before me like a child,
A child at play, a wind-excited bird.

    A ghost from the soul's house?
    I'm where I always was.
    The lily broods. Who knows
    The way out of a rose?

2

Is it the sea we wish? The sleep of the changeless?
In my left ear I hear the loud sound of a minor collapse.
Last night I dreamt of a jauntier principle of order;
Today I eat my usual diet of shadows.

Dare I speak, once more, in the monotony of great praise,
In the wild disordered language of the natural heart?
What else can I steal from sleep?

We start from the dark. Pain teaches us little.
I can't laugh from a crater of burning pitch,
Or live the dangerous life of an insect.
Is there a wisdom in objects? Few objects praise the Lord.
The bulks cannot hide us, or the bleak sheds of our desolation,
I know the cold fleshless kiss of contraries,
The nerveless constriction of surfaces—
Machines, machines, loveless, temporal;
Mutilated souls in cold morgues of obligation.

3

There are times when reality comes closer:
In a field, in the actual air,
I stepped carefully, like a new-shod horse,
A raw tumultuous girl
Making my way over wet stones.
And then I ran—
Ran ahead of myself,
Across a field, into a little wood.

And there I stayed until the day burned down.

My breath grew less. I listened like a beast.
Was it the stones I heard? I stared at the fixed stars.

The moon, a pure Islamic shape, looked down.
The light air slowed: It was not night or day.
All natural shapes became symbolical.
The only thing alive in heaven's eye,
I shed my clothes to slow my daemon down.
And then I ran again.

    Where was I going? Where?
    What was I running from?
    To these I cried my life—
    The loved fox, and the wren.

Speech passed between small birds;
Silence became a thing;
Echo itself consumed;
The scene shrank to a pin.

Did my will die? Did I?
I said farewell to sighs,
Once to the toad,
Once to the frog,
And once to my flowing thighs.

Who can believe the moon?
I have seen! I have seen!—
The line! The holy line!
A small place all in flame.

Out, out, you secret beasts,
You birds, you western birds.
One follows fire. One does.
My breath is more than yours.

What lover keeps his song?
I sigh before I sing.
I love because I am
A rapt thing with a name.

4

Ask all the mice who caper in the straw—
I am benign in my own company.
A shape without a shade, or almost none,
I hum in pure vibration, like a saw.
The grandeur of a crazy one alone!—
By swoops of bird, by leaps of fish, I live.
My shadow steadies in a shifting stream;
I live in air; the long light is my home;
I dare caress the stones, the field my friend;
A light wind rises: I become the wind.

FOURTH MEDITATION

1

I was always one for being alone,
Seeking in my own way, eternal purpose;
At the edge of the field waiting for the pure moment;
Standing, silent, on sandy beaches or walking along green embankments;
Knowing the sinuousness of small waters:
As a chip or shell, floating lazily with a slow current,
A drop of the night rain still in me,
A bit of water caught in a wrinkled crevice,
A pool riding and shining with the river,
Dipping up and down in the ripples,
Tilting back the sunlight.

Was it yesterday I stretched out the thin bones of my innocence?
O the songs we hide, singing only to ourselves!
Once I could touch my shadow, and be happy;
In the white kingdoms, I was light as a seed,
Drifting with the blossoms,
A pensive petal.

But a time comes when the vague life of the mouth no longer suffices;
The dead make more impossible demands from their silence;
The soul stands, lonely in its choice,
Waiting, itself a slow thing,
In the changing body.

> The river moves, wrinkled by midges,
> A light wind stirs in the pine needles.
> The shape of a lark rises from a stone;
> But there is no song.

What is it to be a woman?
To be contained, to be a vessel?
To prefer a window to a door?
A pool to a river?
To become lost in a love,
Yet remain only half aware of the intransient glory?
To be a mouth, a meal of meat?
To gaze at a face with the fixed eyes of a spaniel?

I think of the self-involved:
The ritualists of the mirror, the lonely drinkers,
The minions of benzedrine and paraldehyde,
And those who submerge themselves deliberately in trivia,
Women who become their possessions,
Shapes stiffening into metal,
Match-makers, arrangers of picnics—
What do their lives mean,
And the lives of their children?—
The young, brow-beaten early into a baleful silence,
Frozen by a father's lip, a mother's failure to answer.
Have they seen, ever, the sharp bones of the poor?
Or known, once, the soul's authentic hunger,
Those cat-like immaculate creatures
For whom the world works?

What do they need?
O more than a roaring boy,
For the sleek captains of intuition cannot reach them;
They feel neither the tearing iron
Nor the sound of another footstep—
How I wish them awake!
May the high flower of the hay climb into their hearts;
May they lean into light and live;
May they sleep in robes of green, among the ancient ferns;
May their eyes gleam with the first dawn;
May the sun gild them a worm;
May they be taken by the true burning;
May they flame into being!—
I see them as figures walking in a greeny garden,
Their gait formal and elaborate, their hair a glory,
The gentle and beautiful still-to-be-born;

The descendants of the playful tree-shrew that survived the archaic
    killers,
The fang and the claw, the club and the knout, the irrational edict,
The fury of the hate-driven zealot, the meanness of the human weasel;
Who turned a corner in time, when at last he grew a thumb;
A prince of small beginnings, enduring the slow stretches of change,
Who spoke first in the coarse short-hand of the subliminal depths,
Made from his terror and dismay a grave philosophical language;
A lion of flame, pressed to the point of love,
Yet moves gently among the birds.

3

Younglings, the small fish keep heading into the current.
What's become of care? This lake breathes like a rose.
Beguile me, change. What have I fallen from?
I drink my tears in a place where all light comes.
I'm in love with the dead! My whole forehead's a noise!
On a dark day I walk straight toward the rain.
Who else sweats light from a stone?
By singing we defend;
The husk lives on, ardent as a seed;
My back creaks with the dawn.

Is my body speaking? I breathe what I am:
The first and last of all things.
Near the graves of the great dead,
Even the stones speak.

WHAT CAN I TELL MY BONES?

1

Beginner,
Perpetual beginner,
The soul knows not what to believe,
In its small folds, stirring sluggishly,
In the least place of its life,
A pulse beyond nothingness,
A fearful ignorance.

Before the moon draws back,
Dare I blaze like a tree?

In a world always late afternoon,
In the circular smells of a slow wind,
I listen to the weeds' vesperal whine,
Longing for absolutes that never come.
And shapes make me afraid:
The dance of natural objects in the mind,
The immediate sheen, the reality of straw,
The shadows crawling down a sunny wall.

A bird sings out in solitariness
A thin harsh song. The day dies in a child.
How close we are to the sad animals!
I need a pool; I need a puddle's calm.

O my bones,
Beware those perpetual beginnings,
Thinning the soul's substance;
The swan's dread of the darkening shore,
Or these insects pulsing near my skin,
The songs from a spiral tree.

Fury of wind, and no apparent wind,
A gust blowing the leaves suddenly upward,
A vine lashing in dry fury,
A man chasing a cat,
With a broken umbrella,
Crying softly.

It is difficult to say all things are well,
When the worst is about to arrive;
It is fatal to woo yourself,
However graceful the posture.

Loved heart, what can I say?
When I was a lark, I sang;
When I was a worm, I devoured.

The self says, I am;
The heart says, I am less;
The spirit says, you are nothing.

Mist alters the rocks. What can I tell my bones?
My desire's a wind trapped in a cave.
The spirit declares itself to these rocks.
I'm a small stone, loose in the shale.
Love is my wound.

The wide streams go their way,
The pond lapses back into a glassy silence.
The cause of God in me—has it gone?
Do these bones live? Can I live with these bones?
Mother, mother of us all, tell me where I am!
O to be delivered from the rational into the realm of pure song,
My face on fire, close to the points of a star,
A learned nimble girl,
Not drearily bewitched,
But sweetly daft.

To try to become like God
Is far from becoming God.
O, but I seek and care!

I rock in my own dark,
Thinking, God has need of me.
The dead love the unborn.

3

Weeds turn toward the wind weed-skeletons.
How slowly all things alter.
Existence dares perpetuate a soul,
A wedge of heaven's light, autumnal song.
I hear a beat of birds, the plangent wings
That disappear into a waning moon;
The barest speech of light among the stones.

    To what more vast permission have I come?
    When I walk past a vat, water joggles,
    I no longer cry for green in the midst of cinders,
    Or dream of the dead, and their holes.
    Mercy has many arms.

Instead of a devil with horns, I prefer a serpent with scales;
In temptation, I rarely seek counsel;
A prisoner of smells, I would rather eat than pray.
I'm released from the dreary dance of opposites.
The wind rocks with my wish; the rain shields me;
I live in light's extreme; I stretch in all directions;
Sometimes I think I'm several.

    The sun! The sun! And all we can become!
    And the time ripe for running to the moon!
    In the long fields, I leave my father's eye;
    And shake the secrets from my deepest bones;
    My spirit rises with the rising wind;
    I'm thick with leaves and tender as a dove,
    I take the liberties a short life permits—
    I seek my own meekness;
    I recover my tenderness by long looking.
    By midnight I love everything alive.
    Who took the darkness from the air?
    I'm wet with another life.
    Yea, I have gone and stayed.

    What came to me vaguely is now clear,
    As if released by a spirit,
    Or agency outside me.
    Unprayed-for,
    And final.

from I AM! SAYS THE LAMB

1961

Nonsense Poems

THE KITTY-CAT BIRD

The Kitty-Cat Bird, he sat on a Fence.
Said the Wren, your Song isn't worth 10¢.
You're a Fake, you're a Fraud, you're a Hor-rid Pretense!
  —Said the Wren to the Kitty-Cat Bird.

You've too many Tunes, and none of them Good:
I wish you would act like a bird really should,
Or stay by yourself down deep in the wood,
  —Said the Wren to the Kitty-Cat Bird.

You mew like a Cat, you grate like a Jay:
You squeak like a Mouse that's lost in the Hay,
I wouldn't be You for even a day,
  —Said the Wren to the Kitty-Cat Bird.

The Kitty-Cat Bird, he moped and he cried.
Then a real cat came with a Mouth so Wide,
That the Kitty-Cat Bird just hopped inside;
"At last I'm myself!"—and he up and died
  —Did the Kitty—the Kitty-Cat Bird.

You'd better not laugh; and don't say, "Pooh!"
Until you have thought this Sad Tale through:
Be sure that whatever you are is you
  —Or you'll end like the Kitty-Cat Bird.

THE WHALE

There was a most Monstrous Whale:
He had no Skin, he had no Tail.
When he tried to Spout, that Great Big Lubber,
The best he could do was Jiggle his Blubber.

THE YAK

There was a most odious Yak
Who took only toads on his Back:
If you asked for a Ride,
He would act very Snide,
And go humping off, yicketty-yak.

THE DONKEY

I had a Donkey, that was all right,
But he always wanted to fly my Kite;
Every time I let him, the String would bust.
Your Donkey is better behaved, I trust.

THE CEILING

Suppose the Ceiling went Outside
And then caught Cold and Up and Died?
The only Thing we'd have for Proof
That he was Gone, would be the Roof;
I think it would be Most Revealing
To find out how the Ceiling's Feeling.

THE CHAIR

A funny thing about a Chair:
You hardly ever think it's *there*.
To know a Chair is really it,
You sometimes have to go and sit.

172

MYRTLE

There once was a girl named Myrtle
Who, strangely enough, *was* a Turtle:
She was mad as a Hare,
She could growl like a Bear,—
O Nobody understood Myrtle!

She would sit with a Book on her Knees,—
My Poetry-Book, if you please,—
She'd Rant and She'd Roar:
"This stuff is a Bore!
Why I could do better
With only ONE Letter,—
These Poets, they write like *I* Sneeze!"

MYRTLE'S COUSIN

And then there was Myrtle's Cousin,
Who *Always* did Things by the Dozen;
She would Eat at one Glup
Boiled Eggs from a Cup,—
Oh that Cousin! Her Manners! At Lunches!

She'd Dunk and She'd Gubble:
She *was* so much Trouble;
And then without even a Spoon,
She'd *Muddle* the Whole Afternoon
What her Friends *Couldn't* Eat at those Lunches!

GOO-GIRL

Poor Myrtle would sigh, "Sweet my Coz,
The *Things* you do, Nobody does:
Putting Egg in your Shoe
And then making Goo,
Which, with Slobbers and Snorts,
You drink up in Quarts;
And that Gravy and Fat
All over your Hat,—
How *Did* you do *That?*
When you Slurp and go, Poof!
The Cat runs for a Roof
Clear under the Chair;
And your Friends,—how they Stare!
The Mere Mention of Soups
Makes them Huddle in Groups,—
And they'll soon stay away in Great Bunches!"

THE GNU

There's *this* to Remember about the Gnu:
He *closely* Resembles—but I *can't* tell *you!*

THE MONOTONY SONG

A donkey's tail is very nice
You mustn't pull it more than twice,
Now that's a piece of good advice
   —Heigho, meet Hugh and Harry!

One day Hugh walked up to a bear
And said, Old Boy, you're shedding hair,
And shedding more than here and there,
   —Heigho, we're Hugh and Harry!

The bear said, Sir, you go too far,
I wonder who you think you are
To make remarks about my—Grrrr!
   —And there was only Harry!

This Harry ran straight up a wall,
But found he wasn't there at all,
And so he had a horrid fall.
   —Alas, alack for Harry!

My sweetheart is a ugly witch,
And you should see her noses twitch,—
But Goodness Me, her father's rich!
   —And I'm not Hugh nor Harry!

This is, you see, a silly song
And you can sing it all day long—
You'll find I'm either right or wrong
   —Heigho Hugh and Harry!

The moral is, I guess you keep
Yourself awake until you sleep,
And sometimes look before you leap
   —Unless you're Hugh or Harry!

PHILANDER

A Man named Philander S. Goo
Said, "I *know* my Legs Add up to Two!
But I count up to One,
And think I am Done!—
Oh What! Oh what what can I DO?"

THE HIPPO

A Head or Tail—which does he lack?
I think his Forward's coming back!
He lives on Carrots, Leeks and Hay;
He starts to yawn—it takes All Day—

Some time I think I'll live that way.

THE BOY AND THE BUSH

A Boy who had Gumption and Push
Would frequently Talk to a Bush,
And the Bush would say, "Mac,
I'd like to Talk Back,
If I thought you could Hear in a Hush."

Now Nobody Sniggered and Mocked
As Those Two quietly Talked,
Because Nobody Heard,
Not a Beast, Not a Bird,—
So they Talked and they Talked and they Talked.

THE LAMB

The Lamb just says, I AM!
He frisks and whisks, *He* can.
He jumps all over. Who
Are *you?* You're jumping too!

THE LIZARD

> The Time to Tickle a Lizard,
> Is Before, or Right After, a Blizzard.
> Now the place to begin
> Is just under his Chin,—
> And here's more Advice:
> Don't Poke more than Twice
> At an Intimate Place like his Gizzard.

THE WAGTAIL
(For J.S., his son)

> Who knows how the Wag-tail woos?
> Is it a case of just pick and choose?
> Has he Grubs for his Fair?—
> Does he poise in the Air,
> Like a Humming-bird,
> O I've heard!—
> From a crazy old Jack-daw bird
> He comes calling without wiping his Shoes!

THE FAR FIELD

1964

I

North American Sequence

THE LONGING

1

On things asleep, no balm:
A kingdom of stinks and sighs,
Fetor of cockroaches, dead fish, petroleum,
Worse than castoreum of mink or weasels,
Saliva dripping from warm microphones,
Agony of crucifixion on barstools.
        Less and less the illuminated lips,
        Hands active, eyes cherished;
        Happiness left to dogs and children—
        (Matters only a saint mentions!)
Lust fatigues the soul.
How to transcend this sensual emptiness?
(Dreams drain the spirit if we dream too long.)
In a bleak time, when a week of rain is a year,
The slag-heaps fume at the edge of the raw cities:
The gulls wheel over their singular garbage;
The great trees no longer shimmer;
Not even the soot dances.

And the spirit fails to move forward,
But shrinks into a half-life, less than itself,
Falls back, a slug, a loose worm
Ready for any crevice,
An eyeless starer.

2

A wretch needs his wretchedness. Yes.
O pride, thou art a plume upon whose head?

How comprehensive that felicity! . . .
A body with the motion of a soul.
What dream's enough to breathe in? A dark dream.
The rose exceeds, the rose exceeds us all.
Who'd think the moon could pare itself so thin?
A great flame rises from the sunless sea;
The light cries out, and I am there to hear—
I'd be beyond; I'd be beyond the moon,
Bare as a bud, and naked as a worm.

To this extent I'm a stalk.
  —How free; how all alone.
Out of these nothings
  —All beginnings come.

3

I would with the fish, the blackening salmon, and the mad lemmings,
The children dancing, the flowers widening.
Who sighs from far away?
I would unlearn the lingo of exasperation, all the distortions of malice
        and hatred;
I would believe my pain: and the eye quiet on the growing rose;
I would delight in my hands, the branch singing, altering the excessive
        bird;
I long for the imperishable quiet at the heart of form;
I would be a stream, winding between great striated rocks in late
        summer;
A leaf, I would love the leaves, delighting in the redolent disorder of
        this mortal life,
This ambush, this silence,
Where shadow can change into flame,
And the dark be forgotten.
I have left the body of the whale, but the mouth of the night is still
        wide;
On the Bullhead, in the Dakotas, where the eagles eat well,

In the country of few lakes, in the tall buffalo grass at the base of the
    clay buttes,
In the summer heat, I can smell the dead buffalo,
The stench of their damp fur drying in the sun,
The buffalo chips drying.

Old men should be explorers?
I'll be an Indian.
Ogalala?
Iroquois.

MEDITATION AT OYSTER RIVER

1

Over the low, barnacled, elephant-colored rocks,
Come the first tide-ripples, moving, almost without sound, toward
    me,
Running along the narrow furrows of the shore, the rows of dead clam
    shells;
Then a runnel behind me, creeping closer,
Alive with tiny striped fish, and young crabs climbing in and out of
    the water.

No sound from the bay. No violence.
Even the gulls quiet on the far rocks,
Silent, in the deepening light,
Their cat-mewing over,
Their child-whimpering.

At last one long undulant ripple,
Blue-black from where I am sitting,
Makes almost a wave over a barrier of small stones,
Slapping lightly against a sunken log.
I dabble my toes in the brackish foam sliding forward,
Then retire to a rock higher up on the cliff-side.
The wind slackens, light as a moth fanning a stone:
A twilight wind, light as a child's breath
Turning not a leaf, not a ripple.
The dew revives on the beach-grass;
The salt-soaked wood of a fire crackles;
A fish raven turns on its perch (a dead tree in the rivermouth),
Its wings catching a last glint of the reflected sunlight.

2

The self persists like a dying star,
In sleep, afraid. Death's face rises afresh,
Among the shy beasts, the deer at the salt-lick,
The doe with its sloped shoulders loping across the highway,
The young snake, poised in green leaves, waiting for its fly,
The hummingbird, whirring from quince-blossom to morning-glory—

With these I would be.
And with water: the waves coming forward, without cessation,
The waves, altered by sand-bars, beds of kelp, miscellaneous driftwood,
Topped by cross-winds, tugged at by sinuous undercurrents
The tide rustling in, sliding between the ridges of stone,
The tongues of water, creeping in, quietly.

3

In this hour,
In this first heaven of knowing,
The flesh takes on the pure poise of the spirit,
Acquires, for a time, the sandpiper's insouciance,
The hummingbird's surety, the kingfisher's cunning—
I shift on my rock, and I think:
Of the first trembling of a Michigan brook in April,
Over a lip of stone, the tiny rivulet;
And that wrist-thick cascade tumbling from a cleft rock,
Its spray holding a double rain-bow in early morning,
Small enough to be taken in, embraced, by two arms,—
Or the Tittebawasee, in the time between winter and spring,
When the ice melts along the edges in early afternoon.
And the midchannel begins cracking and heaving from the pressure
        beneath,
The ice piling high against the iron-bound spiles,
Gleaming, freezing hard again, creaking at midnight—
And I long for the blast of dynamite,
The sudden sucking roar as the culvert loosens its debris of branches
        and sticks,
Welter of tin cans, pails, old bird nests, a child's shoe riding a log,
As the piled ice breaks away from the battered spiles,
And the whole river begins to move forward, its bridges shaking.

4

Now, in this waning of light,
I rock with the motion of morning;
In the cradle of all that is,
I'm lulled into half-sleep
By the lapping of water,
Cries of the sandpiper.

Water's my will, and my way,
And the spirit runs, intermittently,
In and out of the small waves,
Runs with the intrepid shorebirds—
How graceful the small before danger!

In the first of the moon,
All's a scattering,
A shining.

JOURNEY TO THE INTERIOR

1

In the long journey out of the self,
There are many detours, washed-out interrupted raw places
Where the shale slides dangerously
And the back wheels hang almost over the edge
At the sudden veering, the moment of turning.
Better to hug close, wary of rubble and falling stones.
The arroyo cracking the road, the wind-bitten buttes, the canyons,
Creeks swollen in midsummer from the flash-flood roaring into the
    narrow valley.
Reeds beaten flat by wind and rain,
Grey from the long winter, burnt at the base in late summer.
—Or the path narrowing,
Winding upward toward the stream with its sharp stones,
The upland of alder and birchtrees,
Through the swamp alive with quicksand,
The way blocked at last by a fallen fir-tree,
The thickets darkening,
The ravines ugly.

2

I remember how it was to drive in gravel,
Watching for dangerous down-hill places, where the wheels whined
    beyond eighty—
When you hit the deep pit at the bottom of the swale,
The trick was to throw the car sideways and charge over the hill, full
    of the throttle.
Grinding up and over the narrow road, spitting and roaring.
A chance? Perhaps. But the road was part of me, and its ditches,
And the dust lay thick on my eyelids,—Who ever wore goggles?—
Always a sharp turn to the left past a barn close to the roadside,
To a scurry of small dogs and a shriek of children,
The highway ribboning out in a straight thrust to the North,
To the sand dunes and fish flies, hanging, thicker than moths,
Dying brightly under the street lights sunk in coarse concrete,
The towns with their high pitted road-crowns and deep gutters,

Their wooden stores of silvery pine and weather-beaten red court-
    houses,
An old bridge below with a buckled iron railing, broken by some idiot
    plunger;
Underneath, the sluggish water running between weeds, broken
    wheels, tires, stones.
And all flows past—
The cemetery with two scrubby trees in the middle of the prairie,
The dead snakes and muskrats, the turtles gasping in the rubble,
The spikey purple bushes in the winding dry creek bed—
The floating hawks, the jackrabbits, the grazing cattle—
I am not moving but they are,
And the sun comes out of a blue cloud over the Tetons,
While, farther away, the heat-lightning flashes.
I rise and fall in the slow sea of a grassy plain,
The wind veering the car slightly to the right,
Whipping the line of white laundry, bending the cottonwoods apart,
The scraggly wind-break of a dusty ranch-house.
I rise and fall, and time folds
Into a long moment;
And I hear the lichen speak,
And the ivy advance with its white lizard feet—
On the shimmering road,
On the dusty detour.

3

I see the flower of all water, above and below me, the never receding,
Moving, unmoving in a parched land, white in the moonlight:
The soul at a still-stand,
At ease after rocking the flesh to sleep,
Petals and reflections of petals mixed on the surface of a glassy pool,
And the waves flattening out when the fishermen drag their nets over
    the stones.

In the moment of time when the small drop forms, but does not fall,
I have known the heart of the sun,—
In the dark and light of a dry place,
In a flicker of fire brisked by a dusty wind.
I have heard, in a drip of leaves,
A slight song,
After the midnight cries.

I rehearse myself for this:
The stand at the stretch in the face of death,
Delighting in surface change, the glitter of light on waves,
And I roam elsewhere, my body thinking,
Turning toward the other side of light,
In a tower of wind, a tree idling in air,
Beyond my own echo,
Neither forward nor backward,
Unperplexed, in a place leading nowhere.

As a blind man, lifting a curtain, knows it is morning,
I know this change:
On one side of silence there is no smile;
But when I breathe with the birds,
The spirit of wrath becomes the spirit of blessing,
And the dead begin from their dark to sing in my sleep.

THE LONG WATERS

1

Whether the bees have thoughts, we cannot say,
But the hind part of the worm wiggles the most,
Minnows can hear, and butterflies, yellow and blue,
Rejoice in the language of smells and dancing.
Therefore I reject the world of the dog
Though he hear a note higher than C
And the thrush stopped in the middle of his song.

And I acknowledge my foolishness with God,
My desire for the peaks, the black ravines, the rolling mists
Changing with every twist of wind,
The unsinging fields where no lungs breathe,
Where light is stone.
I return where fire has been,
To the charred edge of the sea
Where the yellowish prongs of grass poke through the blackened ash,
And the bunched logs peel in the afternoon sunlight,
Where the fresh and salt waters meet,
And the sea-winds move through the pine trees,
A country of bays and inlets, and small streams flowing seaward.

2

Mnetha, Mother of Har, protect me
From the worm's advance and retreat, from the butterfly's havoc,
From the slow sinking of the island peninsula, the coral efflorescence,
The dubious sea-change, the heaving sands, and my tentacled sea-
      cousins.

But what of her?—
Who magnifies the morning with her eyes,
That star winking beyond itself,
The cricket-voice deep in the midnight field,
The blue jay rasping from the stunted pine.

How slowly pleasure dies!—
The dry bloom splitting in the wrinkled vale,
The first snow of the year in the dark fir.
Feeling, I still delight in my last fall.

3

In time when the trout and young salmon leap for the low-flying
    insects,
And the ivy-branch, cast to the ground, puts down roots into the saw-
    dust,
And the pine, whole with its roots, sinks into the estuary,
Where it leans, tilted east, a perch for the osprey,
And a fisherman dawdles over a wooden bridge,
These waves, in the sun, remind me of flowers:
The lily's piercing white,
The mottled tiger, best in the corner of a damp place,
The heliotrope, veined like a fish, the persistent morning-glory,
And the bronze of a dead burdock at the edge of a prairie lake,
Down by the muck shrinking to the alkaline center.

I have come here without courting silence,
Blessed by the lips of a low wind,
To a rich desolation of wind and water,
To a landlocked bay, where the salt water is freshened
By small streams running down under fallen fir trees.

4

In the vaporous grey of early morning,
Over the thin, feathery ripples breaking lightly against the irregular
    shoreline—
Feathers of the long swell, burnished, almost oily—
A single wave comes in like the neck of a great swan
Swimming slowly, its back ruffled by the light cross-winds,
To a tree lying flat, its crown half broken.

I remember a stone breaking the eddying current,
Neither white nor red, in the dead middle way,
Where impulse no longer dictates, nor the darkening shadow,
A vulnerable place,
Surrounded by sand, broken shells, the wreckage of water.

5

As light reflects from a lake, in late evening,
When bats fly, close to slightly tilting brownish water,
And the low ripples run over a pebbly shoreline,
As a fire, seemingly long dead, flares up from a downdraft of air in a
        chimney,
Or a breeze moves over the knees from a low hill,
So the sea wind wakes desire.
My body shimmers with a light flame.

I see in the advancing and retreating waters
The shape that came from my sleep, weeping:
The eternal one, the child, the swaying vine branch,
The numinous ring around the opening flower,
The friend that runs before me on the windy headlands,
Neither voice nor vision.

I, who came back from the depths laughing too loudly,
Become another thing;
My eyes extend beyond the farthest bloom of the waves;
I lose and find myself in the long water;
I am gathered together once more;
I embrace the world.

THE FAR FIELD

1

I dream of journeys repeatedly:
Of flying like a bat deep into a narrowing tunnel,
Of driving alone, without luggage, out a long peninsula,
The road lined with snow-laden second growth,
A fine dry snow ticking the windshield,
Alternate snow and sleet, no on-coming traffic,
And no lights behind, in the blurred side-mirror,
The road changing from glazed tarface to a rubble of stone,
Ending at last in a hopeless sand-rut,
Where the car stalls,
Churning in a snowdrift
Until the headlights darken.

2

At the field's end, in the corner missed by the mower,
Where the turf drops off into a grass-hidden culvert,
Haunt of the cat-bird, nesting-place of the field-mouse,
Not too far away from the ever-changing flower-dump,
Among the tin cans, tires, rusted pipes, broken machinery,—
One learned of the eternal;
And in the shrunken face of a dead rat, eaten by rain and ground-
        beetles
(I found it lying among the rubble of an old coal bin)
And the tom-cat, caught near the pheasant-run,
Its entrails strewn over the half-grown flowers,
Blasted to death by the night watchman.

I suffered for birds, for young rabbits caught in the mower,
My grief was not excessive.
For to come upon warblers in early May
Was to forget time and death:
How they filled the oriole's elm, a twittering restless cloud, all one
        morning,
And I watched and watched till my eyes blurred from the bird
        shapes,—
Cape May, Blackburnian, Cerulean,—

Moving, elusive as fish, fearless,
Hanging, bunched like young fruit, bending the end branches,
Still for a moment,
Then pitching away in half-flight,
Lighter than finches,
While the wrens bickered and sang in the half-green hedgerows,
And the flicker drummed from his dead tree in the chicken-yard.

—Or to lie naked in sand,
In the silted shallows of a slow river,
Fingering a shell,
Thinking:
Once I was something like this, mindless,
Or perhaps with another mind, less peculiar;
Or to sink down to the hips in a mossy quagmire;
Or, with skinny knees, to sit astride a wet log,
Believing:
I'll return again,
As a snake or a raucous bird,
Or, with luck, as a lion.

I learned not to fear infinity,
The far field, the windy cliffs of forever,
The dying of time in the white light of tomorrow,
The wheel turning away from itself,
The sprawl of the wave,
The on-coming water.

3

The river turns on itself,
The tree retreats into its own shadow.
I feel a weightless change, a moving forward
As of water quickening before a narrowing channel
When banks converge, and the wide river whitens;
Or when two rivers combine, the blue glacial torrent
And the yellowish-green from the mountainy upland,—
At first a swift rippling between rocks,
Then a long running over flat stones
Before descending to the alluvial plain,
To the clay banks, and the wild grapes hanging from the elmtrees.
The slightly trembling water

Dropping a fine yellow silt where the sun stays;
And the crabs bask near the edge,
The weedy edge, alive with small snakes and bloodsuckers,—
I have come to a still, but not a deep center,
A point outside the glittering current;
My eyes stare at the bottom of a river,
At the irregular stones, iridescent sandgrains,
My mind moves in more than one place,
In a country half-land, half-water.

I am renewed by death, thought of my death,
The dry scent of a dying garden in September,
The wind fanning the ash of a low fire.
What I love is near at hand,
Always, in earth and air.

4

The lost self changes,
Turning toward the sea,
A sea-shape turning around,—
An old man with his feet before the fire,
In robes of green, in garments of adieu.

A man faced with his own immensity
Wakes all the waves, all their loose wandering fire.
The murmur of the absolute, the why
Of being born fails on his naked ears.
His spirit moves like monumental wind
That gentles on a sunny blue plateau.
He is the end of things, the final man.

All finite things reveal infinitude:
The mountain with its singular bright shade
Like the blue shine on freshly frozen snow,
The after-light upon ice-burdened pines;
Odor of basswood on a mountain-slope,
A scent beloved of bees;
Silence of water above a sunken tree:
The pure serene of memory in one man,—
A ripple widening from a single stone
Winding around the waters of the world.

THE ROSE

There are those to whom place is unimportant,
But this place, where sea and fresh water meet,
Is important—
Where the hawks sway out into the wind,
Without a single wingbeat,
And the eagles sail low over the fir trees,
And the gulls cry against the crows
In the curved harbors,
And the tide rises up against the grass
Nibbled by sheep and rabbits.

A time for watching the tide,
For the heron's hieratic fishing,
For the sleepy cries of the towhee,
The morning birds gone, the twittering finches,
But still the flash of the kingfisher, the wingbeat of the scoter,
The sun a ball of fire coming down over the water,
The last geese crossing against the reflected afterlight,
The moon retreating into a vague cloud-shape
To the cries of the owl, the eerie whooper.
The old log subsides with the lessening waves,
And there is silence.

I sway outside myself
Into the darkening currents,
Into the small spillage of driftwood,
The waters swirling past the tiny headlands.
Was it here I wore a crown of birds for a moment
While on a far point of the rocks
The light heightened,
And below, in a mist out of nowhere,
The first rain gathered?

As when a ship sails with a light wind—
The waves less than the ripples made by rising fish,
The lacelike wrinkles of the wake widening, thinning out,
Sliding away from the traveler's eye,
The prow pitching easily up and down,
The whole ship rolling slightly sideways,
The stern high, dipping like a child's boat in a pond—
Our motion continues.

But this rose, this rose in the sea-wind,
Stays,
Stays in its true place,
Flowering out of the dark,
Widening at high noon, face upward,
A single wild rose, struggling out of the white embrace of the morning-
     glory,
Out of the briary hedge, the tangle of matted underbrush,
Beyond the clover, the ragged hay,
Beyond the sea pine, the oak, the wind-tipped madrona,
Moving with the waves, the undulating driftwood,
Where the slow creek winds down to the black sand of the shore
With its thick grassy scum and crabs scuttling back into their
     glistening craters.

And I think of roses, roses,
White and red, in the wide six-hundred-foot greenhouses,
And my father standing astride the cement benches,
Lifting me high over the four-foot stems, the Mrs. Russells, and his
     own elaborate hybrids,
And how those flowerheads seemed to flow toward me, to beckon me,
     only a child, out of myself.

What need for heaven, then,
With that man, and those roses?

What do they tell us, sound and silence?
I think of American sounds in this silence:
On the banks of the Tombstone, the wind-harps having their say,
The thrush singing alone, that easy bird,
The killdeer whistling away from me,
The mimetic chortling of the catbird
Down in the corner of the garden, among the raggedy lilacs,
The bobolink skirring from a broken fencepost,
The bluebird, lover of holes in old wood, lilting its light song,
And that thin cry, like a needle piercing the ear, the insistent cicada,
And the ticking of snow around oil drums in the Dakotas,
The thin whine of telephone wires in the wind of a Michigan winter,
The shriek of nails as old shingles are ripped from the top of a roof,
The bulldozer backing away, the hiss of the sandblaster,
And the deep chorus of horns coming up from the streets in early
        morning.
I return to the twittering of swallows above water,
And that sound, that single sound,
When the mind remembers all,
And gently the light enters the sleeping soul,
A sound so thin it could not woo a bird,

Beautiful my desire, and the place of my desire.

I think of the rock singing, and light making its own silence,
At the edge of a ripening meadow, in early summer,
The moon lolling in the close elm, a shimmer of silver,
Or that lonely time before the breaking of morning
When the slow freight winds along the edge of the ravaged hillside,
And the wind tries the shape of a tree,
While the moon lingers,
And a drop of rain water hangs at the tip of a leaf
Shifting in the wakening sunlight
Like the eye of a new-caught fish.

I live with the rocks, their weeds,
Their filmy fringes of green, their harsh
Edges, their holes
Cut by the sea-slime, far from the crash
Of the long swell,
The oily, tar-laden walls
Of the toppling waves,
Where the salmon ease their way into the kelp beds,
And the sea rearranges itself among the small islands.

Near this rose, in this grove of sun-parched, wind-warped madronas,
Among the half-dead trees, I came upon the true ease of myself,
As if another man appeared out of the depths of my being,
And I stood outside myself,
Beyond becoming and perishing,
A something wholly other,
As if I swayed out on the wildest wave alive,
And yet was still.
And I rejoiced in being what I was:
In the lilac change, the white reptilian calm,
In the bird beyond the bough, the single one
With all the air to greet him as he flies,
The dolphin rising from the darkening waves;

And in this rose, this rose in the sea-wind,
Rooted in stone, keeping the whole of light,
Gathering to itself sound and silence—
Mine and the sea-wind's.

II

Love Poems

THE YOUNG GIRL

What can the spirit believe?—
It takes in the whole body;
I, on coming to love,
Make that my study.

We are one, and yet we are more,
I am told by those who know,—
At times content to be two.
Today I skipped on the shore,
My eyes neither here nor there,
My thin arms to and fro,
A bird my body,
My bird-blood ready.

HER WORDS

A young mouth laughs at a gift.
She croons, like a cat to its claws;
Cries, 'I'm old enough to live
And delight in a lover's praise,
Yet keep to myself my own mind;
I dance to the right, to the left;
My luck raises the wind.'

'Write all my whispers down,'
She cries to her true love.
'I believe, I believe, in the moon!—
What weather of heaven is this?'

'The storm, the storm of a kiss.'

THE APPARITION

My pillow won't tell me
    Where he has gone,
The soft-footed one
    Who passed by, alone.

Who took my heart, whole,
    With a tilt of his eye,
And with it, my soul,
    And it like to die.

I twist, and I turn,
    My breath but a sigh.
Dare I grieve? Dare I mourn?
    He walks by. He walks by.

HER RETICENCE

If I could send him only
One sleeve with my hand in it,
Disembodied, unbloody,
For him to kiss or caress
As he would or would not,—
But never the full look of my eyes,
Nor the whole heart of my thought,
Nor the soul haunting my body,
Nor my lips, my breasts, my thighs
That shiver in the wind
When the wind sighs.

HER LONGING

Before this longing,
I lived serene as a fish,
At one with the plants in the pond,
The mare's tail, the floating frogbit,
Among my eight-legged friends,
Open like a pool, a lesser parsnip,
Like a leech, looping myself along,
A bug-eyed edible one,
A mouth like a stickleback,—
A thing quiescent!

But now—
The wild stream, the sea itself cannot contain me:
I dive with the black hag, the cormorant,
Or walk the pebbly shore with the humpbacked heron,
Shaking out my catch in the morning sunlight,
Or rise with the gar-eagle, the great-winged condor.
Floating over the mountains,
Pitting my breast against the rushing air,
A phoenix, sure of my body,
Perpetually rising out of myself,
My wings hovering over the shorebirds,
Or beating against the black clouds of the storm,
Protecting the sea-cliffs.

HER TIME

When all
My waterfall
Fancies sway away
From me, in the sea's silence;
In the time
When the tide moves
Neither forward nor back,
And the small waves
Begin rising whitely,
And the quick winds
Flick over the close whitecaps,
And two scoters fly low,
Their four wings beating together,
And my salt-laden hair
Flies away from my face
Before the almost invisible
Spray, and the small shapes
Of light on the far
Cliff disappear in a last
Glint of the sun, before
The long surf of the storm booms
Down on the near shore,
When everything—birds, men, dogs—
Runs to cover:
I'm one to follow,
To follow.

SONG

My wrath, where's the edge
Of the fine shapely thought
That I carried so long
When so young, when so young?

My rage, what's to be
The soul's privilege?
Will the heart eat the heart?
What's to come? What's to come?

O love, you who hear
The slow tick of time
In your sea-buried ear,
Tell me now, tell me now.

LIGHT LISTENED

O what could be more nice
Than her ways with a man?
She kissed me more than twice
Once we were left alone.
Who'd look when he could feel?
She'd more sides than a seal.

The close air faintly stirred.
Light deepened to a bell,
The love-beat of a bird.
She kept her body still
And watched the weather flow.
We live by what we do.

All's known, all, all around:
The shape of things to be;
A green thing loves the green
And loves the living ground.
The deep shade gathers night;
She changed with changing light.

We met to leave again
The time we broke from time;
A cold air brought its rain,
The singing of a stem.
She sang a final song;
Light listened when she sang.

Inside, my darling wife
Sharpened a butcher knife;
Sighed out her pure relief
    That I was gone.

When I had tried to clean
My papers up, between
Words skirting the obscene—
    She frowned her frown.

Shelves have a special use;
And Why muddy shoes
In with your underclothes?
    She asked, woman.

So I betook myself
With not one tiny laugh
To drink some half-and-half
    On the back lawn.

Who should come up right then,
But our goose, Marianne,
Having escaped her pen,
    Hunting the sun.

Named for a poetess,
(Whom I like none-the-less),
Her pure-white featheriness
    She paused to preen;

But when she pecked my toe,
My banked-up vertigo
Vanished like April snow;
    All rage was gone.

Then a close towhee, a
Phoebe not far away
Sang out audaciously
    Notes finely drawn.

Back to the house we ran,
Me, and dear Marianne—
Then we romped out again,
    Out again,
    Out again,
    Three in the sun.

HIS FOREBODING

1

The shoal rocks with the sea.
I, living, still abide
The incommensurate dread
Of being, being away
From one comely head.

2

Thought upon thought can be
A burden to the soul.
Who knows the end of it all?
When I pause to talk to a stone,
The dew draws near.

3

I sing the wind around
And hear myself return
To nothingness, alone.
The loneliest thing I know
Is my own mind at play.

4

Is she the all of light?
I sniff the darkening air
And listen to my own feet.
A storm's increasing where
The winds and waters meet.

THE SHY MAN

The full moon was shining upon the broad sea;
I sang to the one star that looked down at me;
I sang to the white horse that grazed on the quay,—
   As I walked by the high sea-wall.
      But my lips they,
      My lips they,
   Said never a word,
   As I moped by the high sea-wall.

The curlew's slow night song came on the water.
That tremble of sweet notes set my heart astir,
As I walked beside her, the O'Connell's daughter,
   I knew that I did love her.
      But my lips they,
      My lips they,
   Said never a word,
   As we walked by the high sea-wall.

The full moon has fallen, the night wind is down
And I lie here thinking in bleak Bofin town
I lie here and thinking, 'I am not alone.'
   For here close beside me is O'Connell's daughter,
      And my lips they, my lips they,
      Say many a word,
   As we embrace by the high sea-wall.
      O! my lips they, my lips they,
      Say many a word,
   As we kiss by the high sea-wall.

HER WRATH

     Dante himself endured,
     And purgatorial ire;
     I, who renew the fire,
     Shiver, and more than twice,
     From another Beatrice.

WISH FOR A YOUNG WIFE

My lizard, my lively writher,
May your limbs never wither,
May the eyes in your face
Survive the green ice
Of envy's mean gaze;
May you live out your life
Without hate, without grief,
And your hair ever blaze,
In the sun, in the sun,
When I am undone,
When I am no one.

III

Mixed Sequence

THE ABYSS

1

Is the stair here?
Where's the stair?
'The stair's right there,
But it goes nowhere.'

And the abyss? the abyss?
'The abyss you can't miss:
It's right where you are—
A step down the stair.'

Each time ever
There always is
Noon of failure,
Part of a house.

In the middle of,
Around a cloud,
On top a thistle
The wind's slowing.

I have been spoken to variously
But heard little.
My inward witness is dismayed
By my unguarded mouth.
I have taken, too often, the dangerous path,
The vague, the arid,
Neither in nor out of this life.

    Among us, who is holy?
    What speech abides?
    I hear the noise of the wall.
    They have declared themselves,
    Those who despise the dove.

Be with me, Whitman, maker of catalogues:
For the world invades me again,
And once more the tongues begin babbling.
And the terrible hunger for objects quails me:
The sill trembles.
And there on the blind
A furred caterpillar crawls down a string.
My symbol!
For I have moved closer to death, lived with death;
Like a nurse he sat with me for weeks, a sly surly attendant,
Watching my hands, wary.
Who sent him away?
I'm no longer a bird dipping a beak into rippling water
But a mole winding through earth,
A night-fishing otter.

3

Too much reality can be a dazzle, a surfeit;
Too close immediacy an exhaustion:
As when the door swings open in a florist's storeroom—
The rush of smells strikes like a cold fire, the throat freezes,
And we turn back to the heat of August,
Chastened.

So the abyss—
The slippery cold heights,
After the blinding misery,
The climbing, the endless turning,
Strike like a fire,
A terrible violence of creation,
A flash into the burning heart of the abominable;
Yet if we wait, unafraid, beyond the fearful instant,
The burning lake turns into a forest pool,
The fire subsides into rings of water,
A sunlit silence.

4

How can I dream except beyond this life?
Can I outleap the sea—
The edge of all the land, the final sea?
I envy the tendrils, their eyeless seeking,
The child's hand reaching into the coiled smilax,
And I obey the wind at my back
Bringing me home from the twilight fishing.

In this, my half-rest,
Knowing slows for a moment,
And not-knowing enters, silent,
Bearing being itself,
And the fire dances
To the stream's
Flowing.

Do we move toward God, or merely another condition?
By the salt waves I hear a river's undersong,
In a place of mottled clouds, a thin mist morning and evening.
I rock between dark and dark,
My soul nearly my own,
My dead selves singing.
And I embrace this calm—
Such quiet under the small leaves!—
Near the stem, whiter at root,
A luminous stillness.

The shade speaks slowly:
'Adore and draw near.
Who knows this—
Knows all.'

5

I thirst by day. I watch by night.
I receive! I have been received!
I hear the flowers drinking in their light,
I have taken counsel of the crab and the sea-urchin,
I recall the falling of small waters,
The stream slipping beneath the mossy logs,
Winding down to the stretch of irregular sand,
The great logs piled like matchsticks.

I am most immoderately married:
The Lord God has taken my heaviness away;
I have merged, like the bird, with the bright air,
And my thought flies to the place by the bo-tree.

Being, not doing, is my first joy.

ELEGY

Her face like a rain-beaten stone on the day she rolled off
With the dark hearse, and enough flowers for an alderman,—
And so she was, in her way, Aunt Tilly.

Sighs, sighs, who says they have sequence?
Between the spirit and the flesh,—what war?
She never knew;
For she asked no quarter and gave none,
Who sat with the dead when the relatives left,
Who fed and tended the infirm, the mad, the epileptic,
And, with a harsh rasp of a laugh at herself,
Faced up to the worst.

I recall how she harried the children away all the late summer
From the one beautiful thing in her yard, the peachtree;
How she kept the wizened, the fallen, the misshapen for herself,
And picked and pickled the best, to be left on rickety doorsteps.

And yet she died in agony,
Her tongue, at the last, thick, black as an ox's.

Terror of cops, bill collectors, betrayers of the poor,—
I see you in some celestial supermarket,
Moving serenely among the leeks and cabbages,
Probing the squash,
Bearing down, with two steady eyes,
On the quaking butcher.

OTTO

1

He was the youngest son of a strange brood,
A Prussian who learned early to be rude
To fools and frauds: He does not put on airs
Who lived above a potting shed for years.
I think of him, and I think of his men,
As close to him as any kith or kin.
Max Laurisch had the greenest thumb of all.
A florist does not woo the beautiful:
He potted plants as if he hated them.
What root of his ever denied its stem?
When flowers grew, their bloom extended him.

2

His hand could fit into a woman's glove,
And in a wood he knew whatever moved;
Once when he saw two poachers on his land,
He threw his rifle over with one hand;
Dry bark flew in their faces from his shot,—
He always knew what he was aiming at.
They stood there with their guns; he walked toward,
Without his rifle, and slapped each one hard;
It was no random act, for those two men
Had slaughtered game, and cut young fir trees down.
I was no more than seven at the time.

3

A house for flowers! House upon house they built,
Whether for love or out of obscure guilt
For ancestors who loved a warlike show,
Or Frenchmen killed a hundred years ago,
And yet still violent men, whose stacked-up guns
Killed every cat that neared their pheasant runs;
When Hattie Wright's angora died as well,
My father took it to her, by the tail.

Who loves the small can be both saint and boor,
(And some grow out of shape, their seed impure;)
The Indians loved him, and the Polish poor.

4

In my mind's eye I see those fields of glass,
As I looked out at them from the high house,
Riding beneath the moon, hid from the moon,
Then slowly breaking whiter in the dawn;
When George the watchman's lantern dropped from sight
The long pipes knocked: it was the end of night.
I'd stand upon my bed, a sleepless child
Watching the waking of my father's world.—
O world so far away! O my lost world!

THE CHUMS

Some are in prison; some are dead;
    And none has read my books,
And yet my thought turns back to them,
    And I remember looks

Their sisters gave me, once or twice;
    But when I slowed my feet,
They taught me not to be too nice
    The way I tipped my hat.

And when I slipped upon the ice,
They saw that I fell more than twice.
    I'm grateful for that.

THE LIZARD

He too has eaten well—
I can see that by the distended pulsing middle;
And his world and mine are the same,
The Mediterranean sun shining on us, equally,
His head, stiff as a scarab, turned to one side,
His right eye staring straight at me,
One leaf-like foot hung laxly
Over the worn curb of the terrace,
The tail straight as an awl,
Then suddenly flung up and over,
Ending curled around and over again,
A thread-like firmness.

(Would a cigarette disturb him?)

At the first scratch of the match
He turns his head slightly,
Retiring to nudge his neck half-way under
A dried strawberry leaf,
His tail grey with the ground now,
One round eye still toward me.
A white cabbage-butterfly drifts in,
Bumbling up and around the bamboo windbreak;
But the eye of the tiny lizard stays with me.
One greenish lid lifts a bit higher,
Then slides down over the eye's surface,
Rising again, slowly,
Opening, closing.

To whom does this terrace belong?—
With its limestone crumbling into fine greyish dust,
Its bevy of bees, and its wind-beaten rickety sun-chairs.
Not to me, but this lizard,
Older than I, or the cockroach.

218

THE MEADOW MOUSE

1

In a shoe box stuffed in an old nylon stocking
Sleeps the baby mouse I found in the meadow,
Where he trembled and shook beneath a stick
Till I caught him up by the tail and brought him in,
Cradled in my hand,
A little quaker, the whole body of him trembling,
His absurd whiskers sticking out like a cartoon-mouse,
His feet like small leaves,
Little lizard-feet,
Whitish and spread wide when he tried to struggle away,
Wriggling like a miniscule puppy.

Now he's eaten his three kinds of cheese and drunk from his bottle-
        cap watering-trough—
So much he just lies in one corner,
His tail curled under him, his belly big
As his head; his bat-like ears
Twitching, tilting toward the least sound.

Do I imagine he no longer trembles
When I come close to him?
He seems no longer to tremble.

2

But this morning the shoe-box house on the back porch is empty.
Where has he gone, my meadow mouse,
My thumb of a child that nuzzled in my palm?—
To run under the hawk's wing,
Under the eye of the great owl watching from the elm-tree,
To live by courtesy of the shrike, the snake, the tom-cat.

I think of the nestling fallen into the deep grass,
The turtle gasping in the dusty rubble of the highway,
The paralytic stunned in the tub, and the water rising,—
All things innocent, hapless, forsaken.

219

HEARD IN A VIOLENT WARD

In heaven, too,
You'd be institutionalized.
But that's all right,—
If they let you eat and swear
With the likes of Blake,
And Christopher Smart,
And that sweet man, John Clare.

THE GERANIUM

When I put her out, once, by the garbage pail,
She looked so limp and bedraggled,
So foolish and trusting, like a sick poodle,
Or a wizened aster in late September,
I brought her back in again
For a new routine—
Vitamins, water, and whatever
Sustenance seemed sensible
At the time: she'd lived
So long on gin, bobbie pins, half-smoked cigars, dead beer,
Her shriveled petals falling
On the faded carpet, the stale
Steak grease stuck to her fuzzy leaves.
(Dried-out, she creaked like a tulip.)

The things she endured!—
The dumb dames shrieking half the night
Or the two of us, alone, both seedy,
Me breathing booze at her,
She leaning out of her pot toward the window.

Near the end, she seemed almost to hear me—
And that was scary—
So when that snuffling cretin of a maid
Threw her, pot and all, into the trash-can,
I said nothing.

But I sacked the presumptuous hag the next week,
I was that lonely.

ON THE QUAY

What they say on the quay is,
   'There's no shelter
From the blow of the wind,
   Or the sea's banter,—
There's two more to drown
   The week after.'

THE STORM
(*Forio d'Ischia*)

1

Against the stone breakwater,
Only an ominous lapping,
While the wind whines overhead,
Coming down from the mountain,
Whistling between the arbors, the winding terraces;
A thin whine of wires, a rattling and flapping of leaves,
And the small street-lamp swinging and slamming against the lamp
    pole.

Where have the people gone?
There is one light on the mountain.

2

Along the sea-wall, a steady sloshing of the swell,
The waves not yet high, but even,
Coming closer and closer upon each other;
A fine fume of rain driving in from the sea,
Riddling the sand, like a wide spray of buckshot,
The wind from the sea and the wind from the mountain contending,
Flicking the foam from the whitecaps straight upward into the dark-
    ness.

A time to go home!—
And a child's dirty shift billows upward out of an alley,
A cat runs from the wind as we do,
Between the whitening trees, up Santa Lucia,
Where the heavy door unlocks,
And our breath comes more easy,—
Then a crack of thunder, and the black rain runs over us, over
The flat-roofed houses, coming down in gusts, beating
The walls, the slatted windows, driving
The last watcher indoors, moving the cardplayers closer
To their cards, their anisette.

222

We creep to our bed, and its straw mattress.
We wait; we listen.
The storm lulls off, then redoubles,
Bending the trees half-way down to the ground,
Shaking loose the last wizened oranges in the orchard,
Flattening the limber carnations.

A spider eases himself down from a swaying light-bulb,
Running over the coverlet, down under the iron bedstead.
The bulb goes on and off, weakly.
Water roars into the cistern.

We lie closer on the gritty pillow,
Breathing heavily, hoping—
For the great last leap of the wave over the breakwater,
The flat boom on the beach of the towering sea-swell,
The sudden shudder as the jutting sea-cliff collapses,
And the hurricane drives the dead straw into the living pine-tree.

THE THING

Suddenly they came flying, like a long scarf of smoke,
Trailing a thing—what was it?—small as a lark
Above the blue air, in the slight haze beyond,
A thing in and out of sight,
Flashing between gold levels of the late sun,
Then throwing itself up and away from the implacable swift pursuers,
Confusing them once flying straight into the sun
So they circled aimlessly for almost a minute,
Only to find, with their long terrible eyes
The small thing diving down toward a hill,
Where they dropped again
In one streak of pursuit.

Then the first bird
Struck;
Then another, another,
Until there was nothing left,
Not even feathers from so far away.

And we turned to our picnic
Of veal soaked in marsala and little larks arranged on a long platter,
And we drank the dry harsh wine
While I poked with a stick at a stone near a four-pronged flower,
And a black bull nudged at a wall in the valley below,
And the blue air darkened.

THE PIKE

The river turns,
Leaving a place for the eye to rest,
A furred, a rocky pool,
A bottom of water.

The crabs tilt and eat, leisurely,
And the small fish lie, without shadow, motionless,
Or drift lazily in and out of the weeds.
The bottom-stones shimmer back their irregular striations,
And the half-sunken branch bends away from the gazer's eye.

A scene for the self to abjure!—
And I lean, almost into the water,
My eye always beyond the surface reflection;
I lean, and love these manifold shapes,
Until, out from a dark cove,
From beyond the end of a mossy log,
With one sinuous ripple, then a rush,
A thrashing-up of the whole pool,
The pike strikes.

ALL MORNING

Here in our aging district the wood pigeon lives with us,
His deep-throated cooing part of the early morning,
Far away, close-at-hand, his call floating over the on-coming traffic,
The lugubriously beautiful plaint uttered at regular intervals,
A protest from the past, a reminder.

They sit, three or four, high in the fir-trees back of the house,
Flapping away heavily when a car blasts too close,
And one drops down to the garden, the high rhododendron,
Only to fly over to his favorite perch, the cross-bar of a telephone pole;
Grave, hieratic, a piece of Assyrian sculpture,
A thing carved of stone or wood, with the dull iridescence of long-
    polished wood,
Looking at you without turning his small head,
With a round vireo's eye, quiet and contained,
Part of the landscape.

And the Steller jay, raucous, sooty headed, lives with us,
Conducting his long wars with the neighborhood cats,
All during mating season,
Making a racket to wake the dead,
To distract attention from the short-tailed ridiculous young ones
Hiding deep in the blackberry bushes—
What a scuttling and rapping along the drainpipes,
A fury of jays, diving and squawking,
When our spayed female cat yawns and stretches out in the sunshine—
And the wrens scold, and the chickadees frisk and frolic,
Pitching lightly over the high hedgerows, dee-deeing,
And the ducks near Lake Washington waddle down the highway after
    a rain,
Stopping traffic, indignant as addled old ladies,
Pecking at crusts and peanuts, their green necks glittering;
And the hummingbird dips in and around the quince tree,
Veering close to my head,
Then whirring off sideways to the top of the hawthorn,
Its almost-invisible wings, buzzing, hitting the loose leaves inter-
    mittently—

A delirium of birds!
Peripheral dippers come to rest on the short grass,
Their heads jod-jodding like pigeons;
The gulls, the gulls far from their waves
Rising, wheeling away with harsh cries,
Coming down on a patch of lawn:

It is neither spring nor summer: it is Always,
With towhees, finches, chickadees, California quail, wood doves,
With wrens, sparrows, juncos, cedar waxwings, flickers,
With Baltimore orioles, Michigan bobolinks,
And those birds forever dead,
The passenger pigeon, the great auk, the Carolina paraquet,
All birds remembered, O never forgotten!
All in my yard, of a perpetual Sunday,
All morning! All morning!

THE MANIFESTATION

Many arrivals make us live: the tree becoming
Green, a bird tipping the topmost bough,
A seed pushing itself beyond itself,
The mole making its way through darkest ground,
The worm, intrepid scholar of the soil—
Do these analogies perplex? A sky with clouds,
The motion of the moon, and waves at play,
A sea-wind pausing in a summer tree.

What does what it should do needs nothing more.
The body moves, though slowly, toward desire.
We come to something without knowing why.

SONG

From whence cometh song?—
From the tear, far away,
From the hound giving tongue,
From the quarry's weak cry.

From whence, love?
From the dirt in the street,
From the bolt, stuck in its groove,
From the cur at my feet.

Whence, death?
From dire hell's mouth,
From the ghost without breath,
The wind shifting south.

THE TRANCED

1

We counted several flames in one small fire.
The question was, Where was the Questioner?—
When we abide yet go
Do we do more than we know,
Or is the body but a motion in a shoe?

2

The edge of heaven was sharper than a sword;
Divinity itself malign, absurd;
Yet love-longing of a kind
Rose up within the mind,
Rose up and fell like an erratic wind.

3

We struggled out of sensuality;
Going, we stayed; and night turned into day;
We paced the living ground;
The stones rang with light sound;
The leaves, the trees turned our two shapes around.

4

Our eyes fixed on a point of light so fine
Subject and object sang and danced as one;
Slowly we moved between
The unseen and the seen,
Our bodies light, and lighted by the moon.

Our small souls hid from their small agonies,
Yet it's the nature of all love to rise:
Being, we came to be
Part of eternity,
And what died with us was the will to die.

THE MOMENT

We passed the ice of pain,
And came to a dark ravine,
And there we sang with the sea:
The wide, the bleak abyss
Shifted with our slow kiss.

Space struggled with time;
The gong of midnight struck
The naked absolute.
Sound, silence sang as one.

All flowed: without, within;
Body met body, we
Created what's to be.

What else to say?
We end in joy.

IV

Sequence, Sometimes Metaphysical

IN A DARK TIME

In a dark time, the eye begins to see,
I meet my shadow in the deepening shade;
I hear my echo in the echoing wood—
A lord of nature weeping to a tree.
I live between the heron and the wren,
Beasts of the hill and serpents of the den.

What's madness but nobility of soul
At odds with circumstance? The day's on fire!
I know the purity of pure despair,
My shadow pinned against a sweating wall.
That place among the rocks—is it a cave,
Or winding path? The edge is what I have.

A steady storm of correspondences!
A night flowing with birds, a ragged moon,
And in broad day the midnight come again!
A man goes far to find out what he is—
Death of the self in a long, tearless night,
All natural shapes blazing unnatural light.

Dark, dark my light, and darker my desire.
My soul, like some heat-maddened summer fly,
Keeps buzzing at the sill. Which I is I?
A fallen man, I climb out of my fear.
The mind enters itself, and God the mind,
And one is One, free in the tearing wind.

IN EVENING AIR

A dark theme keeps me here,
Though summer blazes in the vireo's eye.
Who would be half possessed
By his own nakedness?
Waking's my care—
I'll make a broken music, or I'll die.

Ye littles, lie more close!
Make me, O Lord, a last, a simple thing
Time cannot overwhelm.
Once I transcended time:
A bud broke to a rose,
And I rose from a last diminishing.

I look down the far light
And I behold the dark side of a tree
Far down a billowing plain,
And when I look again,
It's lost upon the night—
Night I embrace, a dear proximity.

I stand by a low fire
Counting the wisps of flame, and I watch how
Light shifts upon the wall.
I bid stillness be still.
I see, in evening air,
How slowly dark comes down on what we do.

THE SEQUEL

1

Was I too glib about eternal things,
An intimate of air and all its songs?
Pure aimlessness pursued and yet pursued
And all wild longings of the insatiate blood
Brought me down to my knees. O who can be
Both moth and flame? The weak moth blundering by.
Whom do we love? I thought I knew the truth;
Of grief I died, but no one knew my death.

2

I saw a body dancing in the wind,
A shape called up out of my natural mind;
I heard a bird stir in its true confine;
A nestling sighed—I called that nestling mine;
A partridge drummed; a minnow nudged its stone;
We danced, we danced, under a dancing moon;
And on the coming of the outrageous dawn,
We danced together, we danced on and on.

3

Morning's a motion in a happy mind:
She stayed in light, as leaves live in the wind,
Swaying in air, like some long water weed.
She left my body, lighter than a seed;
I gave her body full and grave farewell.
A wind came close, like a shy animal.
A light leaf on a tree, she swayed away
To the dark beginnings of another day.

Was nature kind? The heart's core tractable?
All waters waver, and all fires fail.
Leaves, leaves, lean forth and tell me what I am;
This single tree turns into purest flame.
I am a man, a man at intervals
Pacing a room, a room with dead-white walls;
I feel the autumn fail—all that slow fire
Denied in me, who has denied desire.

THE MOTION

1

The soul has many motions, body one.
An old wind-tattered butterfly flew down
And pulsed its wings upon the dusty ground—
Such stretchings of the spirit make no sound.
By lust alone we keep the mind alive,
And grieve into the certainty of love.

2

Love begets love. This torment is my joy.
I watch a river wind itself away;
To meet the world, I rise up in my mind;
I hear a cry and lose it on the wind.
What we put down, must we take up again?
I dare embrace. By striding, I remain.

3

Who but the loved know love's a faring-forth?
Who's old enough to live?—a thing of earth
Knowing how all things alter in the seed
Until they reach this final certitude,
This reach beyond this death, this act of love
In which all creatures share, and thereby live,

4

Wings without feathers creaking in the sun,
The close dirt dancing on a sunless stone
God's night and day: down this space He has smiled,
Hope has its hush: we move through its broad day,—
O who would take the vision from the child?—
O, motion O, our chance is still to be!

INFIRMITY

In purest song one plays the constant fool
As changes shimmer in the inner eye.
I stare and stare into a deepening pool
And tell myself my image cannot die.
I love myself: that's my one constancy.
Oh, to be something else, yet still to be!

Sweet Christ, rejoice in my infirmity;
There's little left I care to call my own.
Today they drained the fluid from a knee
And pumped a shoulder full of cortisone;
Thus I conform to my divinity
By dying inward, like an aging tree.

The instant ages on the living eye;
Light on its rounds, a pure extreme of light
Breaks on me as my meager flesh breaks down—
The soul delights in that extremity.
Blessed the meek; they shall inherit wrath;
I'm son and father of my only death.

A mind too active is no mind at all;
The deep eye sees the shimmer on the stone;
The eternal seeks, and finds, the temporal,
The change from dark to light of the slow moon,
Dead to myself, and all I hold most dear,
I move beyond the reach of wind and fire.

Deep in the greens of summer sing the lives
I've come to love. A vireo whets its bill.
The great day balances upon the leaves;
My ears still hear the bird when all is still;
My soul is still my soul, and still the Son,
And knowing this, I am not yet undone.

Things without hands take hands: there is no choice,—
Eternity's not easily come by.
When opposites come suddenly in place,
I teach my eyes to hear, my ears to see
How body from spirit slowly does unwind
Until we are pure spirit at the end.

THE DECISION

1

What shakes the eye but the invisible?
Running from God's the longest race of all.
A bird kept haunting me when I was young—
The phoebe's slow retreating from its song,
Nor could I put that sound out of my mind,
The sleepy sound of leaves in a light wind.

2

Rising or falling's all one discipline!
The line of my horizon's growing thin!
Which is the way? I cry to the dread black,
The shifting shade, the cinders at my back.
Which is the way? I ask, and turn to go,
As a man turns to face on-coming snow.

THE MARROW

1

The wind from off the sea says nothing new.
The mist above me sings with its small flies.
From a burnt pine the sharp speech of a crow
Tells me my drinking breeds a will to die.
What's the worst portion in this mortal life?
A pensive mistress, and a yelping wife.

2

One white face shimmers brighter than the sun
When contemplation dazzles all I see;
One look too close can take my soul away.
Brooding on God, I may become a man.
Pain wanders through my bones like a lost fire;
What burns me now? Desire, desire, desire.

3

Godhead above my God, are you there still?
To sleep is all my life. In sleep's half-death,
My body alters, altering the soul
That once could melt the dark with its small breath.
Lord, hear me out, and hear me out this day:
From me to Thee's a long and terrible way.

4

I was flung back from suffering and love
When light divided on a storm-tossed tree.
Yea, I have slain my will, and still I live;
I would be near; I shut my eyes to see;
I bleed my bones, their marrow to bestow
Upon that God who knows what I would know.

I WAITED

I waited for the wind to move the dust;
But no wind came.
I seemed to eat the air;
The meadow insects made a level noise.
I rose, a heavy bulk, above the field.

It was as if I tried to walk in hay,
Deep in the mow, and each step deeper down,
Or floated on the surface of a pond,
The slow long ripples winking in my eyes.
I saw all things through water, magnified,
And shimmering. The sun burned through a haze,
And I became all that I looked upon.
I dazzled in the dazzle of a stone.

And then a jackass brayed. A lizard leaped my foot.
Slowly I came back to the dusty road;
And when I walked, my feet seemed deep in sand.
I moved like some heat-weary animal.
I went, not looking back. I was afraid.

The way grew steeper between stony walls,
Then lost itself down through a rocky gorge.
A donkey path led to a small plateau.
Below, the bright sea was, the level waves,
And all the winds came toward me. I was glad.

THE TREE, THE BIRD

Uprose, uprose, the stony fields uprose,
And every snail dipped toward me its pure horn.
The sweet light met me as I walked toward
A small voice calling from a drifting cloud.
I was a finger pointing at the moon,
At ease with joy, a self-enchanted man.
Yet when I sighed, I stood outside my life,
A leaf unaltered by the midnight scene,
Part of a tree still dark, still, deathly still,
Riding the air, a willow with its kind,
Bearing its life and more, a double sound,
Kin to the wind, and the bleak whistling rain.

The willow with its bird grew loud, grew louder still.
I could not bear its song, that altering
With every shift of air, those beating wings,
The lonely buzz behind my midnight eyes;—
How deep the mother-root of that still cry!

The present falls, the present falls away;
How pure the motion of the rising day,
The white sea widening on a farther shore.
The bird, the beating bird, extending wings—.
Thus I endure this last pure stretch of joy,
The dire dimension of a final thing.

THE RESTORED

In a hand like a bowl
Danced my own soul,
Small as an elf,
All by itself.

When she thought I thought
She dropped as if shot.
'I've only one wing,' she said,
'The other's gone dead,'

'I'm maimed; I can't fly;
I'm like to die,'
Cried the soul
From my hand like a bowl.

When I raged, when I wailed,
And my reason failed,
That delicate thing
Grew back a new wing,

And danced, at high noon,
On a hot, dusty stone,
In the still point of light
Of my last midnight.

THE RIGHT THING

Let others probe the mystery if they can.
Time-harried prisoners of *Shall* and *Will*—
The right thing happens to the happy man.

The bird flies out, the bird flies back again;
The hill becomes the valley, and is still;
Let others delve that mystery if they can.

God bless the roots!—Body and soul are one!
The small become the great, the great the small;
The right thing happens to the happy man.

Child of the dark, he can out leap the sun,
His being single, and that being all:
The right thing happens to the happy man.

Or he sits still, a solid figure when
The self-destructive shake the common wall;
Takes to himself what mystery he can,

And, praising change as the slow night comes on,
Wills what he would, surrendering his will
Till mystery is no more: No more he can.
The right thing happens to the happy man.

ONCE MORE, THE ROUND

What's greater, Pebble or Pond?
What can be known? The Unknown.
My true self runs toward a Hill
More! O More! visible.

Now I adore my life
With the Bird, the abiding Leaf,
With the Fish, the questing Snail,
And the Eye altering all;
And I dance with William Blake
For love, for Love's sake;

And everything comes to One,
As we dance on, dance on, dance on.

PREVIOUSLY UNCOLLECTED POEMS

LIGHT POEM

Wren-song in trellis: a light ecstasy of butterflies courting,
Nudging and tickling of ants and spiders,
Flutter of wings and seeds quaking,
Little crabs slipping into watery craters—
All that diving and pitching and swooping.

Liquids pursue me, notes and tremors:
I am undone by the gurgle of babies and pitchers,
A dried stalk in a welter of sinuous grasses,
Wanting the quiet of old wood or stone without water.

MEDITATION IN HYDROTHERAPY

Six hours a day I lay me down
Within this tub but cannot drown.

The ice cap at my rigid neck
Has served to keep me with the quick.

This water, heated like my blood,
Refits me for the true and good.

Within this primal element
The flesh is willing to repent.

I do not laugh; I do not cry;
I'm sweating out the will to die.

My past is sliding down the drain;
I soon will be myself again.

LINES UPON LEAVING A SANITARIUM

Self-contemplation is a curse
That makes an old confusion worse.

Recumbency is unrefined
And leads to errors in the mind.

Long gazing at the ceiling will
In time induce a mental ill.

The mirror tells some truth, but not
Enough to merit constant thought.

He who himself begins to loathe
Grows sick in flesh and spirit both.

Dissection is a virtue when
It operates on other men.

SONG

1

This fair parcel of summer's
Asleep in her skin,
A lark-sweet lover if ever there was.
The fountain
Hangs by its hair;
The water is busy
In the place of beautiful stones.
To the north of a mouth I lie,
Hearing a crass babble of birds.

To find that, like a fish,
What the fat leaves have,—
How else, meadow-shape?

2

That day we took from the angels:
Light stayed all night,
Rocking the blossoms;
The sea barked in its caves.
I sang to the straw,
The likeliest gander alive.

How fast the winsome escapes!
I saw in my last sleep
The stunned country of ourselves.
In the soft slack of a neck I slept.
Her arms made a summer.

Where's the bridge of dancing children?
The edge is what we have.
In the grey otherwise,
The instant gathers.
I'm still,
Still as the wind's center,
Still as a clay sunk
Stone.

Do the dead wake in their own way?
I warm myself with cold.
Redeem this teacher,
Love.

3

Love makes me naked;
Propinquity's a harsh master;
O the songs we hide singing to ourselves!—
Are these matters only a saint mentions?
Am I reduced to the indignity of examples?
I'm still smudgy from sleep:
Flash me to mercy and a whole heart!
Here's the last kiss of my luck:
Dearie, delight me now.
The bird in the small bush
Bewilders himself:

All things are vulnerable, still;
The soul has its own shine and shape;
And the vine climbs;
And the great leaves cancel their stems;
And sinuosity
Saves.

THE CHANGELING

1

She with her thighs harder than hooves,
Turns, mouse-wary,—
By what reminded?
The dark heart of some ancient thing
Stays in her flesh;
Her choices whisper.
Think of the task of air!—
As she steps into summer,
O most manifest.
She leans into light, and lives,
Her heaven-sense pure as a stone.
Long bones are loveliest: I love long bones.

2

A wretch needs his wretchedness. Yes. But this shape
Sways me awake. What ho, and the field's my friend,
And the cyclamen leaves glisten like the backs of baby turtles.
I've recovered my tenderness by long looking;
I'm a Socrates of small fury.
The wave bends with the fish. I'm taught
As water teaches stone. Believe me, extremest oriole,
I can hear light on a dry day.
The world is where we fling it; I'm leaving where I am.
You larks all day, you robins right,
You birds,
Take notice of this man!
My speech must be:
I'll sing beyond the wind
Things of high wit and changes of the moon.

3

Sad the soul's joy. Loved heart, what else can I say
To you arbutus calm, mysterious as a stone?
How is it inside a tree?
I can't bury the bone of this misery like a fastidious dog.
To the best of myself I sing,
While the rock-seams swell with the sea,
And the sun touches the lizard's throat, its tail half in shadow.
Is this fare for the cats and dogs?
It's no dalliance.

Dear sparrows of this alley,
To this extent I'm a stalk.
How free! How all alone!
By light's extreme,
By all the things that are,
I've come to be.

    Apples! Have a care!
    She's coming near!
    Is it to bring the lily?
    Is it to bring
    Birds to this watery air?
    You fishes, be more fond.
    The small! The small!
    I hear them singing!
    Dove utterly,
    Divergent bird,
    The vine winds to its work;
    She with her larchy sweetness,
    Her nails brighter than shells,
    She's come to pierce a cloud!
    To pierce a cloud.
    A cloud.

THE FOLLIES OF ADAM

1

Read me Euripides,
Or some old lout who can
Remember what it was
To jump out of his skin.
Things speak to me, I swear;
But why am I groaning here,
Not even out of breath?

2

What are scepter and crown?
No more than what is raised
By a naked stem:
The rose leaps to this girl;
The earthly lives in her;
A thorn does well in the wind,
At ease with all that flows.

3

I talked to a shrunken root;
Ah, how she laughed to see
Me staring past my foot,
One toe in eternity;
But when the root replied,
She shivered in her skin,
And looked away.

4

Father and son of this death,
The soul dies every night;
In the wide white, the known
Reaches of common day,
What eagle needs a tree?
The flesh fathers a dream;
All true bones sing alone.

5

Poseidon's only a horse,
Laughed a master of hump and snort;
He cared so much for the sport,
He rode all night, and came
Back on the sea-foam;
And when he got to the shore,
He laughed, once more.

THREE EPIGRAMS

1. *Pipling*

Behold the critic, pitched like the *castrati*,
Imperious youngling, though approaching forty;
He heaps few honors on a living head;
He loves himself, and the illustrious dead;
He pipes, he squeaks, he quivers through his nose,—
Some cannot praise him: *I* am one of those.

2. *The Mistake*

He left his pants upon a chair:
She was a widow, so she said:
But he was apprehended, bare,
By one who rose up from the dead.

3. *The Centaur*

The Centaur does not need a Horse;
He's part of one, as a matter of course.
'Twixt animal and man divided,
His sex-life never is one-sided.
He does what Doves and Sparrows do—
What else he does is up to you.

THE HARSH COUNTRY

There was a hardness of stone,
An uncertain glory,
Glitter of basalt and mica,
And the sheen of ravens.

Between cliffs of light
We strayed like children,
Not feeling the coarse shale
That cut like razors,

For a blond hill beckoned
Like an enormous beacon,
Shifting in sea change,
Not ever farther.

Yet for this we travelled
With hope, and not alone,
In the country of ourselves,
In a country of bright stone.

A ROUSE FOR STEVENS

(To Be Sung in a Young Poets' Saloon)

Wallace Stevens, what's he done?
He can play the flitter-flad;
He can see the second sun
Spinning through the lordly cloud.

He's imagination's prince:
He can plink the skitter-bum;
How he rolls the vocables,
Brings the secret—right in Here!

Wallace, Wallace, wo ist er?
Never met him, Dutchman dear;
If I ate and drank like him,
I would be a chanticleer.

(TOGETHER)
Speak it from the face out clearly:
Here's a *mensch* but can sing dandy.
Er ist niemals ausgepoopen,
Altes Wunderkind.

(AUDIENCE)
Roar 'em, whore 'em, cockalorum,
The Muses, they must all adore him,
Wallace Stevens—are we *for* him?
Brother, he's our father!

THE SAGINAW SONG

In Saginaw, in Saginaw,
  The wind blows up your feet,
When the ladies' guild puts on a feed,
  There's beans on every plate,
And if you eat more than you should,
  Destruction is complete.

Out Hemlock Way there is a stream
  That some have called Swan Creek;
The turtles have bloodsucker sores,
  And mossy filthy feet;
The bottoms of migrating ducks
  Come off it much less neat.

In Saginaw, in Saginaw,
  Bartenders think no ill;
But they've ways of indicating when
  You are not acting well:
They throw you through the front plate glass
  And then send you the bill.

The Morleys and the Burrows are
  The aristocracy;
A likely thing for they're no worse
  Than the likes of you or me,—
A picture window's one you can't
  Raise up when you would pee.

In Shaginaw, in Shaginaw
  I went to Shunday Shule;
The only thing I ever learned
  Was called the Golden Rhule,—
But that's enough for any man
  What's not a proper fool.

I took the pledge cards on my bike;
  I helped out with the books;
The stingy members when they signed
  Made with their stingy looks,—
The largest contributions came
  From the town's biggest crooks.

In Saginaw, in Saginaw,
  There's never a household fart,
For if it did occur,
  It would blow the place apart,—
I met a woman who could break wind
  And she is my sweet-heart.

O, I'm the genius of the world,—
  Of that you can be sure,
But alas, alack, and me achin' back,
  I'm often a drunken boor;
But when I die—and that won't be soon—
  I'll sing with dear Tom Moore,
  With that lovely man, Tom Moore.

Coda:

  My father never used a stick,
    He slapped me with his hand;
  He was a Prussian through and through
    And knew how to command;
  I ran behind him every day
    He walked our greenhouse land.

  I saw a figure in a cloud,
    A child upon her breast,
  And it was O, my mother O,
    And she was half-undressed,
  All women, O, are beautiful
    When they are half-undressed.

260

I do not have a fiddle so
   I get myself a stick,
And then I beat upon a can,
   Or pound upon a brick;
And if the meter needs a change
   I give the cat a kick.

   Ooomph dah doodle dah
   Ooomph dah doodle dah
   Ooomph dah doodle dah do.

Whenever I feel it coming on
   I need a morning drink,
I get a stool and sit and stare
   In the slop-pail by the sink;
I lean my head near the brimming edge
   And do not mind the stink.

   Oh, the slop-pail is the place to think
   On the perils of too early drink,—
   Too early drink, too early drink,
   Can bring a good man down.

I went fishing with a pin
   In the dark of an ould spittoon;
Me handkerchee had fallen in
   With more than half a crown.
I stared into the dented hole
   And what do you think I saw?—
A color pure, O pure as gold,
   A color without flaw,
A color without flaw, flaw, flaw,
   A color without flaw.
I stared and stared, and what do you think?
   My thirst came on, and I had to drink.

Indeed I saw a shimmering lake
   Of slime and shining spit,
And I kneeled down and did partake
   A bit of the likes of it.
And it reminded me—But Oh!
   I'll keep my big mouth shut.

It happened O, in Bofin Town,
   The color, my dears, was Guinness brown,
But it had a flavor all its own,
   As I gulped it down, as I gulped it down.
There on my knees, a man of renown,
   I did partake of it, I did partake of it.

   Oh, the slop-pail is the place to think
   On the perils of too early drink,
   Too early drink, too early drink
   Will bring a good man down.

THE REPLY

Bird, bird don't edge me in;
    I've had enough today
    Of your fine-honed lay
That prickles my coarse skin.

I'm neither out nor in
    Before that simple tune
    As cryptic as a rune,
    As round and pure as the moon,
And fresh as salt-drenched skin.

This shivers me; I swear
    A tune so bold and bare,
    Yet fine as maidenhair,
Shakes every sense. I'm five
Times five a man; I breathe
    This sudden random song,
    And, like you, bird, I sing,
    A man, a man alive.

DUET

SHE: O when you were little, you were really big:
Now you run to the money, it's jig, jig, jig;
You're becoming that horror, a two-legged pig

BOTH: —In spite of Soren Kierkegaard.

HE: I'll face all that, and the Divine Absurd:
You be an adverb, I'll be a verb,
I'll spit over my chin and beyond the curb,

BOTH: —And close up that chapter of Kierkegaard.

SHE: We'll sail away from the frightful shore
Of multiple choice and Either/or
To the land where the innocent stretch and snore

BOTH: —With never a thought for Kierkegaard.

SHE: I'm shanty Irish

HE: —And *pissoir* French?

SHE: I'm a roaring girl, an expensive wench,

BOTH: But at least we know one needn't blench
—In fear and trembling, dear Kierkegaard.

SHE: A mistress of Zen, I'll bite your thumb,
I'll jump on your belly, I'll kick your bum
Till you come to the land of Kingdom Come

BOTH: —Far beyond, O Beyond! dear Kierkegaard.

HE: My jug, my honey, my can of beer,

SHE: My ex-existentialist darling dear,

BOTH: Should Dame Anxiety ever come near
We'll give each other a box on the ear,
—In honor of Father Kierkegaard.

SUPPER WITH LINDSAY
(1962)

I deal in wisdom, not in dry desire.
Luck! Luck! that's what I care for in a cage
And what fool wouldn't, when things from sleep
Come easy to the sill, things lost from far away.
Behold, the Moon!—
And it stepped in the room, under his arm,—
Lindsay's I mean: two moons, or even three,
I'd say my face is just as round as his,
And that makes three, counting his face as one.
"What Moon?" he cried, half-turning in mock fury.

And then it spilled:
The sudden light spilled on the floor like cream
From a knocked over churn, and foamed around
Us, under the chair-rungs, toward the cellar door.

"Let's eat!" said Lindsay. "Here we've got the Moon,
We've got the living light, but where's the food?"

"Sure, we still eat," I said. "Enough! Or too much."
—"That means Blake, too?"

                When Lindsay bent his head
Half sideways in the shifting light,
His nose looked even bigger than it was,
And one eye gazed askew. "Why, Blake, he's dead,—
But come to think, they say the same of me."

When he said that, a spidery shape dropped down
A swaying light-cord, then ran half-way back.

"That's never Blake," said Lindsay. "He'd be a worm,
One of those fat ones winding through a rose.
Maybe it's Whitman's spider, I can't tell,
Let's eat before the moonlight all runs out."

So we sat down and ate ourselves a meal,
But what we ate I can't remember quite:
Cornbread and milk, ice cream and more ice cream,
With cold roast beef and coffee for dessert—
Mostly I remember the ice cream.

After a while the light began to wane
And flicker near our legs like kerosene
Burning in sand. "It looks like I should go,"—
And Lindsay heaved himself from my old chair.
"The spider's gone," he said bemusedly.

"Who called me poet of the college yell?
We need a breed that mixes Blake and me,
Heroes and bears, and old philosophers—
John Ransom should be here, and René Char;
Paul Bunyan is part Russian, did you know?—
We're getting closer to it all the time."

I walked him through the grill and out the gate
Past alder lane, and we gabbed there a while.
He shook my hand. "Tell Williams I've been here,
And Robert Frost. They might remember me."

With that, he hitched his pants and humped away.

Index of First Lines

267